Also available in the *Teenage Worrier* series,
and published by Corgi Books

I WAS A TEENAGE WORRIER
THE TEENAGE WORRIER'S GUIDE TO LURVE
THE TEENAGE WORRIER'S GUIDE TO LIFE
THE TEENAGE WORRIER'S PANICK DIARY

Pocket Guides
THE TEENAGE WORRIER'S POCKET GUIDE TO FAMILIES
THE TEENAGE WORRIER'S POCKET GUIDE TO MIND
AND BODY
THE TEENAGE WORRIER'S POCKET GUIDE
TO ROMANCE
THE TEENAGE WORRIER'S POCKET GUIDE TO SUCCESS

THE TEENAGE WORRIER'S WORRY FILES
A CORGI BOOK : 0 552 147168

First publication in Great Britain

Printing History
Corgi edition published 1999

3 5 7 9 10 8 6 4 2

Set in 11¹/₂ pt Linotype Garamond

Corgi Books are published by Transworld Publishers,
61–63 Uxbridge Road, London W5 5SA,
a division of the Random House Group Ltd,
in Australia by Random House Australia (Pty) Ltd,
20 Alfred Street, Milsons Point, Sydney, NSW 2061, Australia,
in New Zealand by Random House New Zealand Ltd,
18 Poland Road, Glenfield, Auckland 10, New Zealand;
and in South Africa by Random House (Pty) Ltd,
Endulini, 5a Jubilee Road, Parktown 2193, South Africa.

Made and printed in Great Britain by
Cox & Wyman Ltd, Reading, Berkshire

THE TEENAGE WORRiER'S

W

"WORRY" FILES

Ros Asquith

as Letty Chubb

CORGI BOOKS

Rat-filled room,
Plague Cottages,
Low-ceilinged, Snivelling Wretches Street,
Mangey Town,
Infinitessimal Dot on Already Minuscule Planet Earth,
Spinning Abandoned in Solar System of Deadly Gases
    and Whirling Rocks, In Extinction Path of Massive
    Asteroid,
Lost in Milky Way,
Universe,
Infinity.

Dearest Reader(s),

It has taken some time to get around to writing you this
letter, and—
    Arrgghflurrrrpsplooooon***!!!gwaaaaackmiaaawo
oooh!
    Sorry. Very sorry about that. I'll start again.
    Er, that was the sound of the chair in which I had
finally made moiself *comfortable, at last successfully*
folding long twiglike legs under self, collapsing into
matchwood following Adored Father's No Problem DIY
repair, and precipitating Yr Favourite Authorene into
spiky, cursing heap on floor. I do not believe Virginia
Woolf, Jane Austin Maestro, George Eliot Etck had to put
up with this sort of thing.
    It might take a minute or two to get going again, I hope
you're not in a hurry to get on with something else. The
flurrpsplooon part was descending El Chubb jamming

hand in large slice of chocolate fudge cake thoughtfully left on floor by Little Brother Benjy as sacrifice to placate the Floor Gods, of whom he is Mortally Afraid. I am borrowing his rume to rite this, because I am Oppressed by mine, it is full of reminders of the Person I Wish To Leave Behind, namely moiself.

This is once again a prob not faced by Virginia Woolf, Jane Austin Allegro Etck Etck.

Oh yes, and the gwaaackmiaawoooh was, first, moi screaming on realization of sitting heavily on Adored Cat Rover, closely followed by sound of Adored Cat reflecting on possible permanent internal injuries that may force replacement of belurved diet of Fatto Catto three times a day with convalescent saucer of warm milk and vitamin tablets.

It has taken some time to get around to writing you this letter.

Why? I hear you all cry, as one.

Well, I spose you may have gathered from my address that I am not in the most buoyant of mudes. My miserable sliver of a life is currently shipwrecked on rocks of glume and rent asunder by foul serpents of despair.

HOWEVER, have decided this will be the year in which El Chubb makes a real effort to GROW UP, stop Worrying about bra size, spotz, cold sores and other superficial gurly Worries and turn attention to serious matters, so that by Jan 1st I will be new, shiny, V. Clever and have forgotten completely about heartless, distracting boyz who threaten to ruin my grate Artistick Emission of being a world-famous film director.

*I have discovered something that may help – an old
diary with nothing filled in except my New Year
resolutions for Last year . . . (one of which, as you are sure
to have guessed, was to keep this diary every day). So, I
have catapulted self out of morose coma and into new
energized sense of well-being. I am going to write
something EVERY DAY in this diary to get myself in
trim for keeping a complete WHOLE diary next year, by
which time I will have spring in my sock (hope).*

*How I long for simple pleasures of childhood when all
we had to think about was scaring ourselves to banana* at
Halloween, scarring ourselves for life with dodgy fireworks
and weeping when the big fat bloke in the red suit only
bought us a wooden jigsaw instead of the flying fairy
Cissy Doll with pink limousine, lavender castle and
boyfrend with real-look leather jacket and washable wig.
Those daze of innocence long gone, I proceed.*

*Here are the New year Resolutions I wrote at the
beginning of this year and have failed to keep for nine
whole months. Will endeavour to improve on this as year
goes on, and note resultz in Diary.*

*What will the next three months hold in store? Will my
true belurved, Adam Stone, return from Los Angeles
realizing he lurved me true all along? Will I make werld-
shattering documentary and be held up as new Tarantino
with SOUL? Will I invent spot kure and become heroine
for millions of teenagers werldwide? READ ON.*

Lurve, Letty Chubb ✕
✕

*NB *I still use 'banana' instead of scary werd about dying that rhymes
with 'breath' that I am still too nervous to write.*

Resolutions

1) Write in this diary every day
Yah, boo, pull other one. Well, you have to start
from somewhere and El Chubb is turning over New
Leaf.

2) Clean teeth twice a day
Not my fault this. Water often not working
properly and bathroom always occupied by groning,
swearing adultz or by small spherical brother Benjy,
standing on loo seat trembling because floor is
trying to eat him.

3) Limit spot, zit and pluke examinations to once every two days
Current rate six times daily. This will be V. Diff,
becos you can get a Himalaya-sized pluke from a
standing start inside 24 hrs, but you have to have
something to aim at. Bathroom situation outlined
above shld also help limit visits.

4) Limit bazoom measuring to once a week
Current rate, twice daily. Might be easier to walk
round with no top on until Boyz stop saying
'Howyadoinmate?'

5) Only measure nose every month instead of weekly

After all, you can do something about plukes, teeth Etck, even do something about bazooms one day thankz to Wonderbra Etck but you can't do much about hooters apart from always standing face-on to people or getting Rich enough for Nose Jobs.

6) Stop reading krap magazines like *Smirk, Weenybop, Teendreems* Etck

Bet they're all written by Really Old People, at least 25, cynically manipulating tender emotions of Teenage Worriers.

7) Read V. Good bukes to improve Mind, starting with *War and Peace*

If doesn't Improve Mind, cld always walk around with buke on head to Improve Posture.

8) Do homewerk on day it's set instead of whole week's werth on Sun at 11 pm

Too obvious to need comment, and too difficult to need comment on persistent failure of same either. Must do better.

9) Improove speling

Indubitoobaloobally.

Phew. Must be better person Etck, Etck...

10) Keep rume tidy
Hope I don't lose these resolutions somewhere in my
rume, like last time.

11) Be nice to Benjy
As long as he's nice to *moi*, of course.

**12) Save every speck of money for Granny
Chubb's Spectacles Endeavour (aiming to buy
her a pair for Christmas)**
Charity begins at home.

13) Stop being superstitious
Arg. Why did I choose this number for that one?
Help, Worry, consult Nostradamus, touch wood,
touch floor six times, fondle lucky rabbit's foot, bow
to mune . . .

**14) As above, cure one nervous habit each
month, starting with having to touch the floor
twice whenever I drop something**
Still, if I do touch the floor twice, remember to
make it look like I keep dropping something, then
at least only I will think I'm mad.

15) Be nice about my mother's paintings
Not strictly telling the truth in a Good Cause can be
justified sometimes, espesh if Only Mother has
Cross To Bear like Adored Father and his Dreamz of
Eldorado, fame and fortune.

16) Ditto about my Adored Father's writing
Not strictly telling the truth in a Good Cause can be
justified sometimes, espesh if Adored Father has
Cross To Bear like Only Mother's Dreamz of The
Perfect Family.

17) Make New frendz
And those who don't like *moi* despite every effort on
the part of El Chubb can jump in lake.

**18) Do not wear same pair of socks more than
once**
Cannot find more than one pair of matching socks so
forced to wash them this evening and hope they dry
on radiator if I can persuade V. Mean Mother to turn
on central heating.

19) Keep Up with World Events
V. Dismayed to hear workers in Russia being paid
in sausages. Suppose they are vegetarians?

**20) Add one new werd to vocabulary each day
as part of on-going Self-Improvement course**
Start tomorrow.

FIRST, HERE IS A BRIEF UPDATE ON MY LIFE . . .

MOI

SCABLET (Freudian slip, must explore festering spotz). I mean, **SCARLETT JANE CHUBB** or **LETTY** (I REFUSE to kowtow to my posh gran's obsession with *Gone with the Wind*, which lumbered me with this V. Embarrassing name. Even if it was the *Titanic* of her day, it has proved to be the iceberg of mine. If I resembled Kate Winslet, all curvy and sensuous, gleaming Etck, I might be able to live up to it).

My appearance: still telegraph pole with only one large protuberance (hooter) topped with wild mat of wholewheat spaghetti (sort of spaghetti pole-on-nose). Mug liberally sprinkled with cold sores, zits and lurking eruptions while picturesquely balanced (like gracefule swallow in flight, ahem) by ears which, shld Dumbo ever see them, wld make him sigh in rapture, 'At last, a kindred spirit.'

UPDATE SKULE . . .

My skule Life still reminds me of hamster on wheel, only slightly less stimulating. Sluggs Comprehensive is trying to pull itself out of the gutter by whipping its deprived urban slum occupants to get more than one GCSE each. So, to instil an atmosphere of Serious Werk and dedication to excellence (as our new head Teacher, Mr Portillo, calls it), they have forced us all to wear dread skule uniform. As a result, loads of kidz have sloped off to Skunks, an even glumier skule, from where you hear gunshots and wailing sirens daily. We at Sluggs, meanwhile, are forced into V. Pale gray shirts with slightly darker grey skirts or trousers. Since my colours are fog and ebony, this does not Worry *moi* (akshully I am slightly relieved of Fashion Worries as a result. At least it's one less thing to have to Worry about each morning: should I wear the ebony or the jet T-shirt? Or shld I put on the mist-colour tracksuit bottoms with a hint of smog?)

My boredom (or living banana) with skule life, has led me to make Big Decision to concentrate V.V. Hard on my Film-making career. I have enrolled once more in the V. Embarrassingly named 'New Directions' (*nude erections – gedditt?*) film course, every Friday night under the guidance of V. Exciting young director who is apparently toast of Rome and has graciously agreed to donate his services, ahem, to help inner city deprived oiks like *moi* learn to use camera. Prof. Alfonso Rosselini (I *think* that's his name, but it might be Bertollici) is, not that I care, rumoured to be V. Seeexy.

I will throw *moi*self into this and aim to make V. Imp three-minute film to enter for New Directions Film Competition, thereby winning fame and

12

fortune for *moi*self, I mean for poor suffering family.
If it doesn't werk out, I may return to second
strategy, which is to enrol V. Kwick as a nun (before
I have to take my GCSEs).

UPDATE MOTHER . . .
Alice Constance Gosling

My Only Mother is still V. Anxious to give up her
job at the kiddies' Library. She finds it a V. Sad Fact
that kids only want to read horror, murder mysteries
or soppy romances (just like adults). Her low point
came last week when she organized byootiful display
of Grate Writers' werks from Victorian period to
present day, hoping assembled nine-yr-olds wld
faint with joy at watercolours of fairy picnics, only
to find them all huddled together next to pic of
Frankenstein and asking if he was related to R.L.
Stein, author of *Goosebumps*.

My poor mum was brought up so posh she's never
got used to living without servants picking up her
every whim. If only, she feels, she'd become a Grate
Artist, instead of abandoning her talents to raise a
family (have a feeling there is a lesson for us all in
there somewhere, if only we were not stupid enough
to fall in lurve).

13

UPDATE FATHER . . .
Leonard Anthony Chubb

My Adored Father continues to moulder away,
occasionally hacking out Do-It-Yourself articles (his
own pathetic attempts are littered all over house,
with result that our home is major safety hazard)
and playing GOD II on the computer. GOD II involves
creating several solar systems and then peopling
them with ecologically sound planets kindly to life.
Getting rid of noxious gases, placing them not too
near or too far from stars and creating balance for
life is obv V. Tricky, as he has not yet got a planet
that will allow even an amoeba to develop on it. But
apparently when you do, you get to Level One and a
Heavenly host of Angels with vast bazooms appears
on-screen to sing yr praises. There are four hundred
and eighty-seven levels to get to the point where the
dinosaurs arrive, so I'm not sure whether the Garden
of Eden, which is the next game up, will ever be in
his possession (you can't play it till you have the
Secret Code revealed in level 487). Worst of all, he
has ground to a complete halt on his New Novel,
claiming that it is impossible to be a True Artiste
when surrounded by the caterwauling of Family Life
in the 21st century and that he longs for the days
when Men were Men and cld go out and hack their
novels from the coalface while women did the
cooking, cleaning, child-rearing, shopping,
accounts . . .

UPDATE BROTHER 1 . . .
Ashley (18)

My V. Clever, handsome, talented, kind, saintly
(pass sick bag) brother still ardently pursues noble
learning at Oxford, where he will graduate from to
become Brain Surgeon, werld ruler Etck.

UPDATE BROTHER 2 . . .
Benjy (5)

Benjy, face of cherub, mind of Dr Eville, still comes
into my bed every other night suffering from nit
mares (Yes, dear reader, headlice still visit this house
on regular basis). His most recent terror is that the
incredibly cosy 'welcome' mat my Adored Father
nailed to floor in hall with special purpose of
comforting Benjy, is in fact a trapdoor that will
open to whisk him down toxic aluminium passage
into shark-infested underwater cavern presided over
by leering arch-villain who cackles, 'Aha, Meeester
Chubb, I have been expecting you.'

Teechers never care that Teenage Worriers like
moi are knackered not cos we have been out
cavorting in klubs with eville drugges but cos our
baby brothers are weeping into our pillows or our
old cats are sneezing all night.

Which brings me to . . .

UPDATE PETS . . .
Rover, Horace, Kitty

Rover: constant companion of
my bedchamber. It is to
Rover that I turn in times
of need. I am V. Allergic
to her, but wld rather
have cuddles that make
eyes glow like beacons
and gush like geysers
than no cuddles at all
(sob, self pity, whail of
banshees, heart-breaking sigh
of violins . . .)

Rover: Cat of Cats

   Horace: Benjy's V. Noisy gerbil. Boring, but
nevertheless preferable to **Kitty**, his cute, fluffy ball
of venom, who is definitely an alien from a
malevolent Yuniverse disguised as a kitten.

UPDATE GRANDMOTHERS . . .
Granny Chubb

Until retirement at 75 my dad's mum was a cleaner,
toiling round the homes of slobs like *moi*. She still
gleams as pure example of Lurve, truth, justice and
nobility on this lonesome planet. If werld leaders
were like Granny Chubb there wld be no wars and
peace and harmony wld reign as we all co-existed in
bliss for ever. But I am V. Sad to report that the

werst thing in my life at time of writing (apart from no news of Adam Stone . . . sob, wail) is that Granny Chubb has returned to her postage stamp of a council flat after arguing with my Only Mother about how to cook sprouts. I am currently saving all my spare dosh for my GCSE (Granny Chubb Specs Endeavour) to buy her a decent pair of glasses, so she stops feeding cat food to Benjy and choccy to Rover.

Grandma Gosling

My mother's mother has sadly not improved. Although her lifestyle severely reduced from vast mansion and servants, she still behaves as if we are all oiks who she can't possibly be related to. She is even beginning to include my poor mother in this, as though by marrying a pauper she somehow lost the right to be a Gosling.

UPDATE FRENDZ . . .

Aggy – vertically and horizontally challenged, myopic, brilliantly brainy Aggy is my Best frend at Sluggs. Her flighty white mum ran off with a postman leaving Aggy's kindly black dad in charge of Aggy and hordes of brothers and sisters. Aggy lives in hope her mum will return to nest . . . a hope that the tragick behaviour of werld leaders and other consenting adults does not lead El Chubb to share.

My Best frend out of skule is still gorgeous golden-wigged, vast orbed (eyes as well as bazoomz)

19

Hazel, most byootiful gurl in universe, who despite being pursued by every bloke who passes within 50 miles of her orbit, is in lurve with Mandy, a gurl. This fact is only known to four people: Hazel, Mandy, Aggy and *moi*. I am sworn to secrecy as Hazel's rich Tory parents wld go ballistic (she thinks) if they knew.

My two best friends represent two big things lacking in *moi* (sob): *Brains* (Aggy) and *Beauty* (Hazel).

UPDATE BOYFRENDZ . . .

Brian Bolt

Clever spotty nerdy Brian is the only boy who has ever lurved me. I try to interest him in needlework or space travel or anything that wld get him out of my hair, to no avail.

Daniel Hope

Is now happily ensconsed with my one-time frend, groovy loose-limbed Ozzie temptress, Spiggy, and seems to me to be V. Dull. I can't forgive him for trying to win me back and messing up my relationship with Adam. He speaks with forked tongue.

Adam Stone

I am doing my best to forget his blackberry curls
and winsome smile, his noble ambitions, and lissom
limbs. It is V. Hard, dear reader, V. Haaaard. But he
has not written once, despite my anguished letters
explaining the dreadful misunderstandings that
caused him to race off to Los Angeles to work for
mega-director Mogul Mogul Junior the Third. I
imagine he is now in the arms of Mogul's scheming
daughter, Candice Cleavage (sorry, that should be
Candice Carthage), and whispering sweet
somethings to her even as I write . . . arg. My love
for him burns with steadfast flame, despite his
rejection. Sometimes I looong to weep on my
mother's shoulder, but – I never told my folks about
Adam, and anyway my Only Mother is too busy
trying to be Leonarda da Vinci. Rover is V.
Sympathetick though.

UPDATES ON ECCENTRICITIES ETCK . . .

This year I will try to get a grip on my Bad Habitz,
otherwise I think a life as a nun is the only option.
After all, nuns pray a lot at odd moments and there
is usually no-one around to see them when they do
all the other odd things, like fringe-twisting,
touching things twice, stroking Lucky Rabbit's foot
Etck. I'm not sure if many nuns are as scared as I am
of that word that is about dying and rhymes with

'breath' though, as they have to confront these matters anyway and are sure that when their time comes they will be whisked up in golden chariot by Heavenly Host & Co which must be V. Comforting. Anyway, I still use 'banana' for this as none of my other experiments have werked. I tried to get closer by using 'deaf' once, but even that made me nervous and when I used it in an essay I just got a spelling correction and had to look at the DREAD word itself, written out in RED INK. This made me queasy all day. Of course, in skulewerk I usually use phrases like 'untimely end' or 'breathed their last' but the sense of melodrama is not always embraced by the teacher, specially when writing about beansprouts.

Thurs Oct 1

Saw best-luking boy have ever seen in LIFE today.

SPOKE to him too.

Was in Gurlz Loo at Sluggs, smothered in Marmite.

Usual pathetick start to day. Combed through post on doormat, just ten-day old leaflets for Indian takeaways and pizza deliveries, unpaid bills, tasteful neo-Georgian aluminium windows Etck, in hopeless search for letter from Adam. Cldn't get into bathroom because of mad family examining hairlines, bags under eyes, colour of waste products, threat posed by floor pattern Etck, so nearly weed self on bus and was obliged to hurtle into loo on arrival at skule, with seconds to spare before lessons supervised as usual by staff of Broadmoor, dogs owned by men in black vests and shades, Spanish Inquisition Etck.

Note with despair tousled wig, not as in Recently Tousled by Rampant Tousler in designer underpants eating designer ice-cream, but as in porcupine hit by speeding truck. Clutching flapping homewerk rescued from gerbil's nest, run into best-luking boy have ever seen coming out of said Gurlz Loo.

Frozen to spot like vole hypnotized by cobra, rabbit in headlights, Innocent Yoof realizing for first time what Adored Parents Akshully Did to create them . . .

Attempt to lean casually against doorpost but miss, banging head on door and dropping homewerk in bucket of Flash unfortunately left outside loo by janitor after cleaning same, not before. Wave away anxious attentions of Mystery Boy, accidentally hitting him in right eye, causing him to stagger back into dinnerlady wheeling trolley full of cottage pies, but fortunately no time for recriminations as aforesaid lady no sooner flung prone onto vehicle of ghastly comestibles before latter whizzes off down corridor due to impact of Sid Snoggs and Frendz who have shot round corner at speed of Escaping Felons in *The Bill*, which is what they're cut out to be, mark wordz of El Chubb.

Mystery Boy blushes at Visage of El Chubb, mistaking overwhelming LUST for disapproval, but poss also influenced by implications of deafening crashing sound in distance as speeding cottage pie trolley and passenger reach point of no return. Shouting above the din, the following intimate, no-holds-barred conversation follows:

Him: Sorry. Thought it was the Boyz.
Me: Myaahsplurfnnnnaaaahhahaha. (I often find I say this on such occasions. It's hard to know what I mean by it, but it fills embarrassing silences – OK, with embarrassing noises.)
Him: No, don't be cross, really, a mistake. Honest.
Me: Nyaaark. Splafffft. Yukkanurk . . .
Him (backing away): Really sorry.

Me: No, don't Worry, it's fine. Mistake anyone could make. Come back. Come in. Who cares?

This last bit is what I wish I had said of course. In Real Life was so gobsmacked I just stood with mouth open squeaking faintly. However, I could swear, I think, that he cast me a Significant Glance as he departed. You know, ghost-of-smile hovering round sculpted smacker, hint-of-smoulder beaming laser-like from under forest of lashes . . .

Rest of day V. Normal and boring, except for visit of ambulance to remove dinnerlady, and industrial cleaners in race against time to hose impacted cottage pies off walls of Year Seven classroom at end of corridor before inmates licked same spotless and all died in horrible agony. Kept thinking I would see Mystery Boy again, but No. Trouble with V. Big skules like Sluggs is you can move about for daze without seeing a single familiar face except yr own tutor group. Anyway, he *could* even be a student teacher, as looks, um, V. Mature . . .

Quizzed Aggy furiously, at first opportunity, which was Library lesson, but she hadn't seen him. Exchange between me and Aggy went something like this:

  'Have you SEEEEEEN that new boy?'
  'Eh?'
  'Oh, nothing, just peachiest boy on planet.'
  'Huh?'

'Aggy, couldn't you just for once stop discovering the Meaning of the Universe, put that buke down and look me in the eye and tell me if you've seen that, that hunk, before.'

(Aggy sighs, puts down buke, adjusts pebble specs and gazes wearily but with unmistakable hint of affection at El Chubb.) 'Letty, I don't know what you're talking about. What's he look like?'

'Well, about five feet 10 inches tall, eyes a mix of sea-green and ocean blue, very dark but with flecks of gold in, you know, a bit like a sea tossed by the wind with floating specks of sand catching the glinting sunlight. Soft hair about this long, thick, the colour of, of (YES) – vanilla fudge, a straight nose, about this long and with just the teeniest little bump in the middle, chiselled type jaw but, you know, not boringly chiselled like Action Man, with a curly sort of mouth in a half smile, a little dimpled cleft on either side, a long neck but not too long. Um, broad shoulders tapering to a narrow waist with a neat bum, you know, but quite pert and long legs, very straight. Complexion the colour of (YES) – toffee fudge. Oh, and a tiny scar on his left cheek, in the shape of a lightning flash. Not that I had that long to take him in, as it were . . .'

'I'll need more to go on than that.'

But, she agreed to keep her eyes peeled and returned to reading Stephen Hawkings's *A Brief History of Time*. I flipped idly through the men's underwear ads in some Krap Mag and wondered whether a buke on the subject might bring Fame and Fortune to *moi*, as well as Deep Interlekshual Cred if it were called *A Timely History of Briefs*. Cursed lack of knowledge about serious matters, vulnerability to charms of opposite sex, superficiality Etck. How can I be so pathetick when only yesterday I swore that my lurve for Adam Stone was all that mattered?

Still, who is this boy? Why is he here? Four weeks into the term? And, if he akshully is in sixth form, why would anyone CHOOSE Sluggs to do A levels when 98% of pupils surge off to DHSS or welfare-to-werk schemes the minute they hit sixteen? Hmmmmmm. A mystery.

Ponder on this as I write, curled up in Granny Chubb's bolero with Rover and hot water-bottle. Too tired to do homewerk now. Will just have kwick, last look at *Smirk* before throwing out all krap magazines and starting *War and Peace*.

My film course is tomorrow.

Glad to have discovered Mystery Boy, because he might prevent me getting crush on renowned sex-bomb, I mean admired Film tutor Alfonso Rossini, and thus avoiding tragick previous experiences re Getting Things about teachers. Will enable *moi* to concentrate on the V. Important techniques of Faction.

NB **Faction: Exciting New Werd**. Means mix of fact and fiction. Have decided to tell Granny Chubb's story in grainy black and white stills, but will jazz it up with Tarantino style bludde and guts for Blitz scenes. Wonder if local butcher would provide bucket or two of spare animal bitz for same? Reluctantly conclude that though vibrations of El Chubb puking might provide authentic war-zone camera shake, general misery might not be worth it.

Fri Oct 2
Film Course, 7.30

Woke up V. Twitchy about Film course. I was so humiliated last term . . . Still, at least it's unlikely any of same people will be there, since they were all dilettantes. (This is a V. Good **new werd**, meaning people who flit about not taking anything seriously, unlike *moi*. I wld not mind being a dilettante, though one wld have to be careful it didn't take up too much time, arf arf.)

Only Mother still groning re period pains and crashing round kitchen. 'Breakfast' of dry biscuit and water accompanied by following exchanges in no particular order:

'Why does no-one but me EVER go NEAR a shop? You know, to do SHOPPING?'

'Shopping? You haven't seen the inside of anything except your own head and the off-licence for months.'

'There's nothing in the fridge but a mildewed muffin and a fossilized frankfurter.'

'That's not the fridge. And it's not a frankfurter.' Close examination followed by triumphant exclamation: 'It's a fish finger.'

'This is no way to bring up kids.'

'Poor Benjy and the cats will starve.'

(NB Reader please note: *Benjy and the CATS will starve*, NOT *Letty will starve*. This confirms my suspicion that once you stop being Cute and turn into a Teenage Worrier Nobody Cares.)

'Just as well he gets a decent skule dinner.'

'Don't want hobble skule dinner. Dog poo. Want packed lunch.'

'You get packed lunch over my dead body.'

Sound of Benjy treating this statement as a promise, and making machine gun noises at mother . . .

Father lurches off to corner shop and arrives back with six newspapers, a tin of rottyerlungs double-strength tobacco and bottle of milk.

'I've married a man with the brain of an ant. You get newspapers and DRUGS. WHERE's the FOOD?'

'We're not married. We need milk, since

unfortunately the resident cow doesn't provide any. Anyway, ants are very bright.'

And so on.

I serenely retrieve undone homewerk from clutches of Horace, who is about to shred same, and exit, Worrying about my skule uniform. Supposing I meet Mystery Boy on bus? Shld I have worn a darker grey? Shld my shirt be tucked in or left tantalizingly loose? So much for abandoning Fashion Worries.

Absolutely No Sign of Mystery Boy all day long.

Am beginning to wonder if he was figment of my fevered imagination.

Werse, maybe he was pervert preying on Gurlz' loos who had decided to defy convention and not wear usual pervert's uniform of dirty raincoat, trousers with missing fly, stubble, bluddeshot leer, underarm stains, furry tongue, stooping walk Etck. (It is a V. Disconcerting part of becoming a Groan-Up to realize people with V. Dodgy thingz on their minds do not look the way they do in Fairy Stories, viz, to whit Hollywood Movies.) Arg. If this is the case, shld I report it to Ms Farthing? Have, of course, found it difficult to report anything to Ms Farthing since my Adored Father inadvertently omitted the 'h' from her name in a sick note. She now believes me to be from dysfunctional family. Perhaps with reason. Worry, Worry.

Syd Snoggs put chewing gum on my chair and so have to wear shirt tantalizingly loose on way home in order to cover up vast glob of gum stuck indelibly to bum. Do not notice anyone being tantalized.

Home to stunning meal of fish fingers, frozen peas and oven chips both burned and soggy, no mean feet even for Only Mother, who is unusually gifted in this Dept. Wonder if ours is only house where home cooking is werse than skule food? Feel deep surge of anguished grief for brief period when Granny Chubb was in residence baking apple pies. Will add learning to cook to list of resolutions . . .

Only Mother complains that if she spent time cooking it wld only be wasted as we never eat anything fancy. I suggest that in order to enjoy fancy food you have to akshully have tasted it, and what about experimenting with, say, a little avocado salad?

'Can I 'ave a car dough?' pipes up Benjy.

'It's a pear.'

'Can I 'ave two car doughs then?'

'Oh Benjy. *What* a clever joke.'

Benjy baffled by this praise. Sometimes I don't understand my mum. She goes up the wall and across the ceiling one minute cos Benjy hasn't yet been taught to read Charles Dickens backwards in medieval French, the next she thinks he ought to have his own chat show cos he's stuck a bit of pasta onto some green card and called it a rain forest, or he knows what a pair is (as a matter of fact, he knows more than one version of what a pair is, but I'm not so sure Only Mother wld be so happy about that).

Still, bite lip to keep resolutions of being V. Nice to Only Family (lucky to have one, some people have had their entire families disappear down loo, get sucked into dustcarts, be blown to bits by their own fartz so they have to live in cardboard boxes, eat mud, moisten parched lips with drainwater and so on) and address self to Major Issue of what to Wear at Film Course. Realize have left it V. Late and so opt for coal-black top, jet-black trousers, soot-black plastic belt and reckless dab of hair gel.

'I see Beetnics are back' murmurs Adored Father, casting glumey glance at my outfit as I lurch from house with V. Neat briefcase-style portfolio of photos, notepad Etck. Thinks: wot is Beetnic? Must look this up and add to vocabulary.

Journey to Film Course involves bus and tube, but have left 40 mins, so shld be fine.

Four buses arrived cuddling each other. Obviously my Lucky Star shineth tonite. Am whisked on wings of escalator into bowels of tube, while octogenarian busker plays *My Way* on banjo with one string missing and the others out of tune. Ruefully throw my last minto to him, which he attempts by reflex to catch in his teeth before remembering he doesn't have any, minto whizzes down creaking windpipe and nearly kills Anciente Minstrel in apoplectic coughing fit, thus delaying El Chubb with emergency revival technique, viz banging him furiously on scrawny back before being accosted by station staff accusing *moi* of mugging helpless and unfortunate member of underclarse.

Continue journey pondering decision never to carry money at night due to Mugging Worry. Wld prefer of course not to carry entire Bod at night and frequently at other times of the day, due to Mugging Worry, and await invention of machine that can fax you whole to yr destination with interest. V. Clever Computer Enhancement techniques shld make it possible to subtly improve appearance of Bod *en route*.

V. Excited at taking tube to more salubrious area of throbbing metropolis, see how other half live (or more to point, other seventh??) because of course the proportion of the population akshully waving big-spender credit cards around, living in houses with three loos and things called *en suite* bathrooms is V. Small. But though small, this group is V. Magnetic for everyone else, who want to peer into the tinted

34

windows of their Lives as they flash past us on fast track Etck.

Pondering these thoughts, El Chubb hurtles straight into first available carriage, only to realize as doors hissed shut that train is going in opposite direction to desired destination. Arg. Had just calculated with lightning brain-speed that turnaround time from next stop will only add four minutes to journey when eerie creaking and shuddering signalled that tube had other ideas.

There is nothing so still as a London tube when you are in a hurry and it is stuck. There is nothing so beige as the raincoats of your fellow sufferers, nothing so glumey as their poor tragick faces, each caught in its own little patch of personal misery.

The glume of the tube

One is thinking, 'I'll miss *MunnyGrubbers* and never know whether Petunia from Teignmouth got a million quid.' Another, 'I'll miss the connection and my true lurve will get fed up waiting and go off with that boilermaker from Slough.' Another, 'I'm sure I can smell smoke, this is Ye Ende.' Only the tramp slumped in corner with a dog on string carrying can of lager round its neck seems not to notice whether train is going anywhere or not.

Moi? Moi is thinking, 'That Alfonso Rustleini (or whatever he's called) will not think me a Serious Person if I can't even turn up on time for the first day of the course.' Descent into Deep Self Pity interrupted by tramp waking up and breaking into loud rendering of *Show Me the Way to Go Home* in noble attempt to cheer stony-faced fellow travellers.

Feel Idea coming on. Maybe I cld make V. Good mean streets documentary-type film about the *tube*. Can still link it to Granny Chubb story by interposing gharstley War pix with deeply glumey tube pix. This V. Brilliant Idea in fact, as suddenly recall that during the Blitz people used to shelter in underground stations. SO, cld use V. Old people, winos Etck on tube today, all sad and isolated and intercut with warm community spirit of air-raid shelters when everyone helped everyone else. Film wld ask questions about 'War and Peace' (will start reading same tomorrow), nature of Life, what we are doing to help pensioners, can we find Lurve in the Darke Corners of Life? Etck.

Tube arrives at station at last. Race across platform at lightning speed only to wait fifteen minutes for tube in other direction to sounds of whirring station announcement: *We are sorry for delays on the zgplfft line, this is due to mxbnvjjjvt at boooiiiiiiiinggggggg plook. Passengers wishing to travel to blung twerdle shld take the bus to znt and change. Other passengers should wait on platform pppppppplllllllllllrtz for further announcements.*

Station announcements always sound as if they're being spoken by Evil Bloke from *Superman* who could only be sent back to His home galaxy by tricking him into saying his name backwards, but of course they never send you to yr Home Galaxy but in totally wrong direction, or in no direction at all. Making station announcements audible will be one of El Chubb's first tasks on becoming Prime Minister.

It was 7.45 when I got off the tube, arg, mone, whinge, humiliation, GLUME. 8.00 when I found the place (it was so flash I walked past it four times, looking for a grotty old pile like the last film course's building), and 8.15 before I found the right room in the maze of gleaming corridors, polished steel, shimmering glass Etck that made up the Flash Escape Studio. Attempting to round up herd of buffaloes stampeding in Brane, I timidly pushed open the emerald glass doors to behold sight so amazing that I was, well, amazed.

This was a Palace of Wonder. Walls, floors and ceilings were covered by huge grainy black and white stills from Grate Movies, parallel lines of black perspex tables streamed endlessly down centre of rume, surrounded by cameras, lights Etck and peopled by rows of cool looking people clad in black from head to foot. Stood blinking like rabbit in headlights. Was attempting to send V. Slow-moving message from Brane to legs consisting of the single word 'Run', when heard 'Meez Cherrrbb, I prezoooooooom' intoned in husky Italian tones.

Alfonso Bertolucci was taking the register (having been late himself owing to Art Movie première), but it was nothing like taking the register as performed at Sluggs Comprehensive – glumey teachers intoning names like reading war dead, voices offering suggestions like 'She's gone to the hospital because her head's fallen off, miss' or 'He's got his thing stuck in the bathroom keyhole and they're waiting for the fire brigade, sir.' To get us all in the mood, Alfredo Fettucini had arranged for a film crew to capture his every move, and was reading out the names in V. Dramatique voice, almost invisible in shadow save for eerie lighting emphasizing arty cheekbones, penetrating eyes Etck.

This was different enough, but what followed, unlike my previous experience, was the most V. Interesting lekture I have ever had privilege to be part of. Suddenly realized I had never been well taught in my whole LIFE before. Alphonso Musclekleeni, despite being muffled in vast black cape from head to toe, and sneezing extravagantly into a black silk hanky every 30 seconds ('I ave a

orreeeble eeenglish cold,' he croaked, accusingly)
seemed to range over the whole history of film in
the next two hours. And he finally sent us whirling
out into dark streets full of enthusiasm for New
Dawn Etck.

Brane of Arresto Artyluni is vast mountain of
intellect compared to puny gnat-sized inhabitant of
L.Chubb's own nut. Am totally INSPIRED.

List of things to do for next class:

1) **Spend every spare minute on tube taking
   pix.**
2) **Spend every other spare minute taking pix
   of Granny Chubb.**
3) **Spend every other spare minute in library
   reading film bukes.**

Next week he is going to tell us how to do
professional storyboard based on ideas we bring.
Week after that, he is going to choose the best six
stories and we are akshully going to MAKE them
into three-minute real filmz over the following
weeks. And the best will win ONE THOUSAND
QUID. I can't believe it. Wot is truly grate is that
there are only 20 people in the class and even
though, from wot I cld tell in strange lighting Etck,
they are all V. Interlekshual types, it does give me a
speck of a chance. Er, nearly one in three I calculate
with speed of lumbago afflicted tortoise.

NB **New Werd: lumbago.** Back pain. V. Pleased

with new werd rate although couldn't find 'Beetnic' in dictionary. Was forced to ask Adored Father who said *Beatniks* were weirdos in 1950s who hung about coffee bars in black polo necks and shades. Nothing new there, then.

Fell into bed at midnight after short shouting match with Only Mother who was staying up Worrying about *moi*. Knackered, but cup overfloweth with JOY (And for once, not cos of BOY).

Sat Oct 3
Write to Adam.

7 **am**. Woken by alarm that I forgot to turn off last night. Arg. Still, joyz of film course come flooding into nut. I put the above note to *moi*self in yesterday morning but am now too involved in my grate werk as Artiste to think about writing to Adam. Will spend entire day down tube, armed with only father's ancient Leica (V. Good 35mm single lens reflex number as used by grate photo-artiste Henri Cartier Bresson, so there. I always cover it in black tape, just like Bresson did, so then the silver bits won't flash and people won't notice *moi* sneaking *You've Been Framed* style pix of them). Just have a little snooze first, as don't want to disturb softly slumbering Rover.

12.30 Have just been woken by irate Only Mother. 'Are you festering in bed all day what about homewerk, tidying room, Grandma Gosling coming to lunch?' Etck. Arg. Had forgotten about dread visit of Gosling, who only flaps down to London once in blue moon, thank God, but it means I can't exactly slink off when she does. Mother exits throwing six letters on my bed.

'I know it's none of my business,' she remarks, 'but just WHO is Adam Stone?'

You have heard, dear reader, of hearts skipping a beat. You have doubtless experienced it for yourself. As have I. But the number of beats skipped by my heart in those few seconds it took to grab the letters came close to cutting off essential supplies even to low-power 15-watt brane.

He had written.

Not once, not twice, but SIX times. They must have been held up in the post by some grisly calamity. Probably the fault of the horrible postman that ran off with Aggy's mother. Couldn't believe it. Tears sprang unbidden to my peepers so that I cld hardly see to tear open the first flimsy airmail missive that leapt into my trembling fingers.

Could just make out that scrawled across the back in big letters was S.W.A.L.K . . . *Sealed With A Loving Kiss*. Swooooon. All thoughts of Mystery Boy, or of poncey interlekshual film tutors with fancy names giving lektures as if they were in *film noir* movies, fled as my sweaty palms unleashed the

41

fluttering letter. Unfolding its voluminous folds and wiping waterfall of tears from cheeks with Rover's tail, I cld think only of Adam.

AAAdaaaaaaaaam Aaaaadaaaaaam Stoooooone . . . his blackberry curls, his winsome limbs, his kind and gentle serious and worthy Soul, now trapped in the vice-like grip of ravening Hollywood and longing only to be entwined once more with mine. The thought of him waiting endlessly for a reply, never daring to phone for fear of rejection, tore at my heart and caused fresh tears to gush on to letter, smudging the bright pink ink. Written in pink. For Lurve. And this is what I read:

> *My dearest beloved Adam,*
> *There has been a terrible mistake.*
> *What you think happened between*
> *me and Daniel Hope never did*
> *happen . . .*

Arg.

Terrible mistake is right.

This was not a letter from Adam to me, but a letter from me to him.

I grabbed the next letter – and the next. Before me lay six letters I had written to him. On the envelopes, as I could now plainly see, was written: RETURN TO SENDER.

How could I have been so stoooopid? How could

42

I have thought that sober, intelligent Adam would write S.W.A.L.K. on a letter? Or do it in PINK INK? How could I have been thick enough to do that *moi*self? He must have been so repelled by them that he couldn't even be bothered to read them. They had been returned unopened.

I will draw a veil over the next half hour, except to say that I now must drag self from bed of sorrow, drag comb through wig, dredge through suppurating pile of socks Etck for something slightly clean to put on for lunch with Granny Gosling. My glume knows no bounds.

11.30 pm. Although have no heart for writing this, cannot sleep, so might as well.

Granny Gosling arrived six minutes early for lunch.

'Scarlett, *darling*. What an *interesting* get-up. Leonard, *isn't* it funny how they dress these days? Can you imagine, what MY grandmother would have said if I'd come down to lunch like that? H-haar di har.' (*Tinkling laugh at pitch to shatter hearing of high flying fruit bat.*) 'What's that, darling? Pigeon? Oh, roast CHICKEN. Gorgeous. What a dear little bird. *So* economical. Can I help with anything? Shell some peas? No, frozen, of *course*. Bread sauce? No bread sauce? Oh, no darling, *course* I don't mind. It's so hard for you, poor Alice, without any HELP. And of *course*, you never had a chance to learn to cook, did you dear, because we had everything all laid on . . .' (*brief pause as she hoovers a tumbler and a half of sherry before onslaught three*). 'Now, Leonard, I've got a simply super idea for raising a little more hard earned *cash*. I *know* you're a WONDERFUL writer, but if you're going to write about shelving couldn't you do it a bit faster, write for several papers at once? Or else be a war correspondent for the *Daily Rant*? If you feel a bit queasy about watching people getting killed, not that it ever did my husband any harm, you could always write about how to put up shelving on walls decimated by shellfire, it would be just the gimmick to make you a fortune, har tee heeeh har.'

'And does that come with life insurance?' muttered Father, smiling benignly through gritted teeth as he carved only roast dinner we have had since last Christmas and imagined the chicken was Gosling except that eating her, though tempting, would have spoiled his appetite. Appetite of El Chubb at low ebb, as I mournfully pushed roast potato round plate attempting to avoid diluting watery gravy further with niagara fall of tears.

'Scarlett, you *are* looking peaky, how's that awful school?'

'Fine.'

'Poor, daaarling Scarlett. Having to go to an Inner London comprehensive. We CAN'T let that happen to *pooooor* little Benjy too.' (Where were we going to move to, I thought, Mars? But on she ploughed.) 'Have you seen those league tables,

Alice? I'm afraid Sluggs comes out very poorly, very poorly indeed. You'll have to pull your socks up, darling, if you're to *shine*. Speaking of which, do you always wear an odd pair? Haaaar ti hi ti hi ti hi.'

Only person unaware of Cold War level of Family Tension was Benjy, who made a mountain of roast spuds and then covered them with ketchup and orange juice, as Grandma Gosling's eyes stretched to their limits.

She then dropped bombshell of asking to see my bedrume. Only Mother waylaid her with lemon drizzle cake (which she shockingly pretended she'd baked herself) while I sprinted round rume on winged boots like bat out of hell doing L. Chubb's famed Tidy-Up Tips. For those of you unfamiliar with previous tomes I repeat them here:

1) **Get Big box.**
2) **Put everything except bed in it.**
3) **Put box under bed.**

Akshully, I had never tried this before and had to get box V. Kwick, which meant I had to empty one of Adored Father's on to his study floor. No grate difference to his floor, which is already invisible for unwashed cups, food remains, items of clothing Etck, like state of local cinema after kids' matinee. The resulting difference to my rume, however, was spectacular and I felt moment of Swelling Pride as The Gosling briefly admired my duvet.

$\mathcal{L}$. Chubb's Famed Tidy-up-tips.

① **<u>GET BIG BOX</u>**

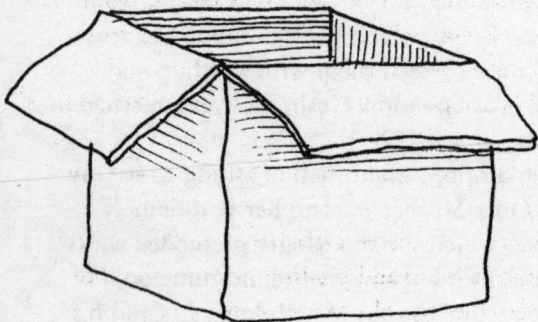

② Put everything except bed in box. Shove box under bed

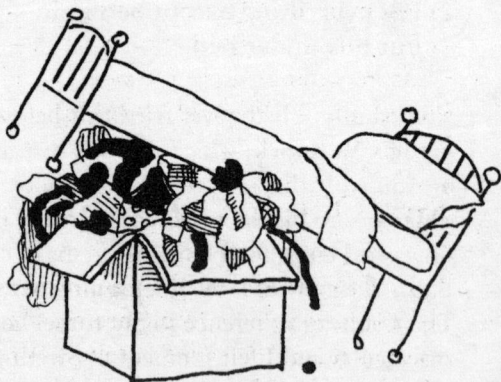

Whoops.

'How sweet, darling, glad to see you're not growing up TOO fast . . .'

(OK, I'll admit it, my duvet has a *My Pretty Puppy* pattern which I've had since I was seven.)

Finding nothing to criticize, the Gosling swept regally out to mone about pokey rumes and didn't my mother miss the rolling parkland of her childhood home and wasn't it a pity we all had to be brought up these daze without at least a field-full of private fresh air to ourselves, and hot and cold running tutors?

Everyone V. Exhausted after her departure and we all lay about groning and picking our noses before treating ourselves to cold roast potato in front of *MunnyGrubbers* in which poor old Ethel Stoat who'd hitch-hiked all the way up from her hovel in Northants to be on the telly, on the very verge of getting a million quid, found herself only with the booby prize: a pack of eazi-stick cup hooks and a two-piece set of aluminium ovenware.

As I cry self to sleep, I wonder, who is more glumey tonite? Poor old Ethel Stoat or *moi*?

Sun Oct 4

3 am. Cannot sleep as Benjy and Rover entwined on bed and anyway poor feeble heart is breaking as result of Adam tragedy. But felt V. Sorry for Benjy when he wobbled in wailing that the patch of carpet just by his bed was a whirlpool and that he had only just avoided being sucked down into raging depths and basted with ketchup and orange juice before being eaten by a horde of grate white sharks with giant knives and forks instead of teeth. I patiently explain it was only a dream. I also told him **V. Interesting Fact**: that more people are killed by coconuts falling on their heads each year than by grate white sharks. I then reminded him that only a few weeks ago he thought the carpet was a quicksand. Then I said I wld go and stand on it to show him it was just a carpet. Bad move.

'Nooooooooooo, noooooooooooo, Lettoooooooooo. Nooooo! OOOOOO will DWOWN. It will thuck oooooo down.'

So I let him stay.

Will now set alarm clock for 8.00 am and whisk off down tube to do photos. Am more determined to stick to this plan than ever as what else is there to live for? (Will also improve SELF by adding New resolution to list, Viz: Learning Interesting New Fact each week.)

11 pm. All is offal, chaff and dross. Why bother with art? What hope is there for young women to fulfil themselves even in so-called era of gurl-power Etck? I was forced to stay in all day with sick Benjy as Only Mother and Father went cavorting off to afternoon DRINKS with his poncey AGENT and didn't return till ten minutes ago. It's not my fault I didn't wake up till 12.30. It's the krap alarm clock.

Benjy and I watched TV for five hrs then made V. Nice Potion, which cheered *moi* up a bit. Potion consisted of: ketchup, breadcrumbs, detergent, mouse droppings (I think), four pints of water with green food colouring in, rotten egg plus shell.

Sometimes having a little brother can be a comfort and keeps you in Touch with the Child Within Yrself. Apparently V. Important, according to interlekshuals like John Cleese Etck. Now I will have to take photos after skule on Mon and Tue, get them done at skule darkroom on Wed, organize folder on Thur. Arg.

V. Upset by loud shouting from parents' rume, along lines of:

'Acting like that at YOUR age . . . disgusting.'
'I *am* acting my age, in case you haven't noticed.'
And on. And on. Arg.

Hope I won't have to bring up Benjy on my own. Wld rather look after Child Within for a little longer, and put off looking after Child Without for as long as possible, espesh one with Floor Phobia, which can make the simplest everyday necessities of life V. Difficult.

Mon Oct 5
Succoth, first day

Also National Book Week. Also National Backpain Week (Arg, Worry re vast numbers of Teenage

Worriers like *moi* who get arthritis from carrying
vast skule bagz full of bukes cos our poor olde skules
can't afford lockers, whinge, Unfair).

7.10 am. NB Must look up 'Succoth' in bid to
understand other kulchures better. V. Big spot on
tip of hooter. Perhaps this is what 'Succoth' meanz.
Must look closely at hooters of fellow citizens today
to see if giant pustular eruptions have broken out all
over Ye Nation, Armed Forces on full alert with
hooter bazookas, remote control robot pluke-pincers,
fleets of crop-dusting planes spraying TCP and other
more noxious fumes . . .

Hold-the-front-page duel-with-destiny question:
does pluke take attention from vast size of hooter?
Or emphasize it?

6.30 pm. Poured heart out to Aggy at lunchtime re
Adam.

'He sent all my letters back . . . (*muffled sobs,
groans, hiccups Etck*) . . . unopened. Can you
beleeeeeeeve it? OOOOh. Aggy. What'll I dooooo?'

Aggy gazed at *moi* in Owlish fashion for some
minutes, suggesting at first she had swallowed four
chicken nuggets simultaneously and become
asphyxiated, or turned to stone at Gorgon-like pop
eyes and snakey wig of El Chubb.

But no, Aggy was leafing through the vast folds
of her cerebellum (have been told it is not the

overall size of brain that matters, so much as its
SURFACE size – and the old brain's only folded all
neatly up in Marks & Sparks clothes dept manner to
keep it safely stowed in protective box of skull,
rather than worn over the outside of one's Bod
frinstance, where it would be vulnerable to attack
from stray objects such as fish and chips, ravenous
hamsters, clutching hands of Syd Snoggs Etck, and
also make one look rather grey and drab, however I
digress . . .). Aggy was leafing through the vast folds
of her hamster-free cerebellum to unlock the
following nugget of info. Viz:

Aggy: What makes you think he's seen them?
Me: Uh?
Aggy: What makes you think Adam has seen your
letters?
Me: He hasn't. I know *that*. He hasn't seen anything
I wrote because he couldn't be bothered to even
open them. He just sent them straight back (*sound of
gulping, more stifled sobz Etck*), proving he doesn't
even CARE enough to . . .
Aggy (*casting weary look as of grate sage addressing
amoeba*): I didn't say 'read', I said 'seen'.
Me: Huh?
Aggy: Maybe he never even got to see the *envelopes*.
Maybe someone else sent them back.
Me: (*faint possibility of hope dawning*): You
mean . . . ??

Of course, once seed of hope sown, my feverish brain ran through myriad possibilities, the two most **salient** (NB **New Werd** meaning significant, important, noteworthy) of which were as follows:

1) Mogul Mogul's vast Empire (to which I had addressed the letters) had about two thousand secretaries, only one of whom knew of young trainee Work-experience-type-Nobody called Adam Stone. V. Difficult for me to stomach thought that young God such as Adam might be seen like this over there in glamorous werld of Hollywood, but I had to admit it was a possibility . . .

2) Mogul Mogul's scheming daughter Candice Carthage had waylaid the mail-person and stolen the letters in frenzy of jealous pashione . . . (I am inclined to take this possibility V. Seriously).

Realize it is POSSIBLE, just POSSIBLE, that Adam really hasn't seen my letters, doesn't know I've written and therefore doesn't think I care.

Resolve to make direct contact with him come hell, high water, plagues of frogs, floors turning into whirlpools Etck, then at least I will KNOW. First things first, must go down tube and take heart-rending photies . . .

11.30 pm. Ugh. Major spoke in wheel of my plans to spend evening taking more heart-rending photies. Was just setting off after tea when heard **dulcet** (NB **New Werd**: meaning 'sweet'. Used in this

case, dear reader, with satyrical intent) tones of
Mother:

'Do hurry, Letty, my appointment's at 7.15 and
we can't afford to get on the wrong side of Ms
Farthing *again*.'

Arg. Had forgotten that this was National Buke
Week, a merry little device supported by skules to
convince anxious parents that their ickle darlings
know which way up to hold buke.

Anyway, it was National Buke Week evening at
Sluggs and my Only Mother insisted on coming and
looking at our 'displays' and chatting animatedly to
teachers about my speling. My Tutor group had
done V. Good display (I thought) about Crime
bukes. There was a V. Brilliant Pop-Up Murder
buke that some kids had done for Benjy's sort of age,
with bodies folding out of cupboards, bludde-
stained machetes springing out at you, ghoulish
laughter sounds (though pressure of time and money
had meant device for this was nicked from old
Christmas card, and was akshully Santa Claus going
'ho ho ho'). And it came with a little plastick knife
to stab into squashy vital organs. Tutor thought
however that the final page, featuring an *LA
Confidential*-style police corruption aspect in form of
cardboard hand extending with envelope full of dosh
might be bad example to younger generation.

My attempts to steer Only Mother towards
werthy project on Grate Artists of the 20th Century
were scuppered by Syd Snoggs, who lurched up

leering and waving gory Murder buke in my
mother's face saying, 'Cor Letty! Didn't know yer
mum was a scorcher. Where you been hiding then,
Mrs Chubb?'

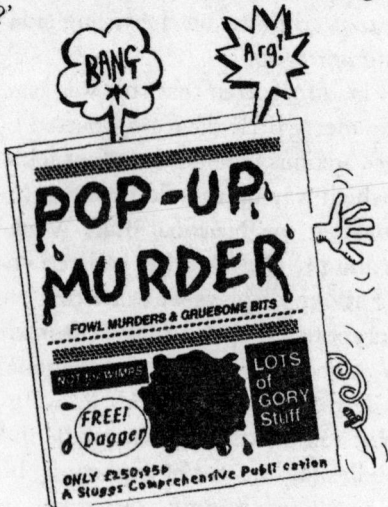

BANG

Arg!

POP-UP
MURDER
FOWL MURDERS & GRUESOME BITS

NOT FOR WIMPS   LOTS
                      of
                      GORY
                      Stuff
FREE!
Dagger

ONLY £250,95p
A Sluggs Comprehensive Publication

Ms Farthing, who has the imagination
of a hamster and the sense of humour of
an ant, said of the above: "Is it about
humane chicken slaughter?"

But Only Mother, instead of hitting him with her
shoulder bag, blushed winsomely and said what
charming manners he had. What has happened to
the fierce feminists of yore, I arsk . . . ?

Whole buke week thing dragged on for hours.
Will draw a veil over tutor's comments about my
werk as being beneath my contempt. Only Mother
and Father thort differently however and had lively

exchange about clarse system, fee-paying skules, collapse of standards Etck, culminating in unkind remarks from my mother to effect that if my dad was so proud of his working-clarse roots why didn't he get off his *un*working-clarse arse and earn enuf for a tutor?

Rang Aggy five mins ago to ask her to ask her big brother's frend if Adam left a forwarding address apart from Mogul's studios. Or if there is a (gasp) telephone number for him. Felt V. Guilty as sobs, wails, Cert-18 curses in V. Squeaky voices in background told *moi* that I had woken most of Aggy's numberless horde of younger siblings.

'Can't get Basil's number now, without waking everyone.'

'Aggy, PLEASE.'

'In the morning. Right?'

(Basil? Oh well, what's in a name?)

Tue Oct 6
Period due.

7.10 am. Spot on nose now size of asteroid from Armageddon. Will Bruce Willys have to tunnel up left nostril, narrowly miss giant bogey avalanche, get almost washed away by torrential waters of impending cold, fight his way out of suffocating folds of Kleenex in order to get rid of it? Will he be in time before El Chubb is totally blotted out by vast hurtling pluke expanding at warp speed, and reduced to infinitessimal fragments Lost in Space?

Giant Plukeoid has now been joined by frolicsome cluster of teeny pimples on chin. I take note of date above – which explains fact that wig seems to have been deep-fried in chicken fat – and wear four winged sanitary pads. Doesn't matter how many wings I wear, though, they never help me catch bus. Today, I *have* to spend evening down tube, taking grate werld-shattering photos.

11.30 pm. You may find this hard to believe, dear Teenage Worriers, but as I was about to leave house this evening armed only with camera and Travel Pass, I heard the dulcet (part of discovering new werds is to use em again kwick so's not to forget) tones of my Only Mother, thus:

'We'll be back about 11, darling. Make sure Benjy's not late to bed.' Followed by slamming of door.

Yeech.

Race downstairs only to see rusty, clanging taped-together health hazard that Father describes as car bumping off round corner exuding life-threatening blue fumes.

How COULD they go out without consulting me? Rushed to kitchen to look at calendar which parents placed there in pathetick attempt to order household chaos. It has been covered by telephone bills, pizza leaflets Etck . . . but on it, tragickally, is ringed *Tue Oct 6th Mum and Dad out. Letty to babysit.*

Only option was to bribe reluctant Benjy to accompany *moi* on journey through London Underground's mean streets.

'No, not goin hobble tube. Watchin video.'

'Either you go to bed RIGHT NOW or you come with me.'

'Go to bed.'

'Ooh, Benjy, dear sweet Benjy, please. It'll be an adventure, you know, like Harrison Ford.'

'Wiv alligators?'

'Well, not exactly . . . but there might be rats. Look, I'll give you a whole pack of Glurgs.'

'Ten packs. An a burger.'

We compromised on four packs of Glurgs plus promise of more to come when funds allowed and possibility of V. Cheap burger, ditto. In return, extracted promise that he wld not tell parents about this, um, adventure . . .

I had V. Good idea of what sort of pix I wanted to represent Soft Underbelly of Unfeeling Metropolis Etck. You know the sort of thing – isolated, hollow-eyed old people in beige cardies, staring ahead of them to avoid locking watery eyes with psychotic tattooed druggies, slumped winos, Etck. To protect Benjy from werst excesses of London's seedy nightlife, I recommended he bring improving buke. I suggested *Fluff the Magic Puppy* or *Apples and Bears ABC*. He chose *Dr Vile and the Crypt of Doom*.

Down into bowels of seething tube we travelled

in search of yuman tragedies that Shame Us All. On it we sat. For two hours. Who was on the tube along with us, I hear you ask?

1) Lots of blokes in suits, reading *Business News*.

2) Lots of women in suits, reading *Business News*.

3) Large party of old folk in beige cardies having sing-along and eating sweets, on way back from London's 'theatreland' having seen matinee of fab new musical called *Whoops! A Vicar in My Soup*. They stuffed Benjy with sweeties and told me off for keeping him up so late, obviously thinking I was irresponsible single parent. I must luke V. Raddled and older than my tender yrs.

4) Lots of V. Squeaky Clean kule-looking kidz in designer labels, unfortunately attached to squeaky clean kule items of clothing, ha-ha, yeech.

Why is it you can't find Tales of Yuman Tragedy and Glume when you really need them? Cld not beleeve how different tube was from nite I travelled alone. Could not spot single squashed can, bit of litter Etck, let alone malnourished dog on string, crack addicts smoking from rolled-up job-rejection notes or shouting crone werthy of Dahl's Chickens or Bill Shakespeere. Obviously this photo-journalism thing is more difficult than I had imagined. Maybe you have to spend some daze looking for good pic?

THEN – at last.

A wino finally got on. I snapped away furiously as he reeled niffily about waving arms like windmill and singing V. Rude stuff with lots of 'f' werds, which made Benjy laugh so much the man even offered him some beer. Brilliant. El Chubb, snapper extraordinaire, waits for le moment critique, when Benjy's happy chortle briefly turns to face of anguish, and lo! What-Chance-Have-They-Got Infant-Alcoholism-Shock-Horror pic is captured for posteriority (must luke up spelling of this new werd sometime). Everyone else in the carriage luking V. Snotty.

Hurtled home at 10.45, dragging weeping starving Benjy. 'Where my burger?' Etck Etck. V. Worried in case parents back early (not that they ever are . . .)

Stuffed some bread and Marmite into mouth Benjy conveniently leaves open to pursue constant complaining, made him kwick hot choccy and read *Fluff the Magic Puppy* four times in fevered attempt to assuage guilt and prevent nightmares involving winos, crypts Etck.

Parents arrived home ten mins ago. Father singing in tones somewhat like wino on tube. Mother hissing furiously. Grone, Worry.

But at least I have my Art.

Wed Oct 7

7.30 am. V. Knackered. Chin pimples have terned into Martian landscape. Period has terned into Niagara Falls. Wig has terned into rainforest during monsoon season, but with monsoon of diesel oil mixed with soy sauce. Benjy had nightmare in which kind looking old lady humming snatches of bouncy melodies from *Whoops! A Vicar in My Soup* was offering him sweeties laced with arsenic and luring him on to carpet whose thick shag-pile tendrils (not sure how long this type of carpet will survive popular vocabulary changes in Western Werld) turned into tentacles of giant octopus. Sometimes wonder if Benjy is the true Artist in this house?

Das Kapital Radio (new station urging workers revolution that you can tune into if you sit under bed and wiggle dials for five hours) reveals amazing news that clever wide boy has invented new perfume sed to smell like fab wild flowers, roses Etck. Thought, 'Just the thing for El Chubb.' But no, this costs £47,750 for one bottle, or should I say, flask . . . (Yes, reader, that was 47 thousand spondoogles).

9.00 pm. Dragged self to skule and had to skip lunch in order to develop film in darkrume. Harvey, the V. Nice technician sed he wld do contact sheets for *moi* to choose which ones to print this evening. Felt V. Confident that I have some V. Good shots.

There were loads of lektures from authors for national buke week: Pullova Offhed came to discuss her Teen Romances, much to the disapproval of Mrs Syntax, head of English, who thinks they make Teenage Gurlz out to be only interested in Lurve, Sex, Boyz, Clothes, Make-up, Pop, the very thort. Queues of Year Seven and Eight gurlz lined up for signed copies, but I am Above All That and chose to go to talk impressively titled *History Meets Fiction* by Prof Nobell, hoping that Mystery Boy might be there, I mean so I cld gain further knowledge of the grate swathes of human suffering as depicted in, ahem, Tolstoy's *War and Peace*, which I will be starting at the weekend.

No sign of Mystery Boy, not that I care, as I have eyes only for Adam again. Dozed off in lekture, and woke to echoing empty hall. Arg. 4.30! Raced to darkrume. Locked. Harvey gone. Must now wait in unspeakable anguish till tomorrow to see pix. How cld I be so stupid? Brain of vole numbed by period . . . Too tired even to contemplate letter to Adam. Will do at weekend.

Bought *Weenybop* to cheer self up. Has V. Compelling cover line: *How to Be Good at Everything*. If the people who write these magazines learnt how to be good at remembering to put in the stuff they say they have, or made it any better than a mixture of the stuff you learn in Gurl Guidz and off a bad episode of *Neighbours* it wld be V. Good Thing for a start.

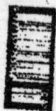

Thurs Oct 8

NB See Resolution 16. Tried to think of something nice to say about Dad's 'novel' but could only find one sheet of writing in Dad's printer. It just said 'Dolores' about twenty times. This V. Worrying. Is Father having male menopause? Arg.

Raced to darkrume V. Early to gaze at contact sheet under beady eye of Harvey, who always gets to skule at crack of dawn.

Heart back in bootz again.

What should have been amazing pix of snarling, grisly wino force-feeding alcohol to frightened child, show cuddly old geezer smiling jovially and apparently offering nice fizzy drink to sweet, eager, smiling Benjy. Obviously le moment *critique* must have been a bit before or a bit after I thought it was. This photography business is harder than it looks. Also had not realized that, without accompanying soundtrack of effing and blinding, the old bloke wld look not only harmless but just like F. Christmas.

Makes you think about importance of sound in movies. Frinstance, you can just have a picture of a door opening and it looks like ad for Door Dept of DIY Superstore. Then add horrible gharstly creaking sounds and sinister squealing violins and it becomes the last crumbling defence before the arrival of mad fiendishly-grinning Jack Nicholson luny bearing Axe.

However, my spirits lightened somewhat as I

examined the pix of nice old ladies on their way back from *Whoops! A Vicar in My Soup*. Two of them look V. Sinister, as are caught in large bat-like shadow of *moi*, looming over them with camera . . .

Harvey thinks I have made a good beginning. Harvey is V. Kind. I sometimes think he is the only person in whole skule who sees the True Artist in *moi* (perhaps it is a shame for the Meeting of Minds that Harvey is about 96 and a grandfather of twelve). Feel twinge of shame as know that if Harvey knew this was not my skulewerk he wld not be so V. Kind and helpful but wld send me off with flea in ear.

Sat late into night writing storyboard to go with pix. Maybe if I can write a convincing enough story, Alfonso Bertolucci might let me have another week in which to get grime and mean tubes effect. Have inserted V. Good ones of Granny Chubb eating straight out of cat food tin and also V. Cherished photo of hers, showing her and Grandpa Chubb digging child out of rubble in Blitz. Needless to say, this last one was not taken by *moi*, but by local newspaper back in 1944.

Mind in whirl re letter to Adam. Was caught composing one during English. Mrs Syntax lumed menacingly above my tremulous frame:

'Scarlett, I see you are doodling hearts all over your work. Is this an integral part of your project?'

'Yes, Mrs Syntax, I believe it is how a young gurl in 1916 would have written to her own true lurve, suffering the torture of the trenches, Miss.'

'I look forward to reading it. With GREAT interest.'

Blurg. Now I've got to write a World War One letter as well as the letter to Adam . . . the crosses I have to bear.

But good news on latter front. Aggy has got phone number for her brother's frend Basil. She sez he is a nice guy who she's known since she was three. He was at playskule with one of her big brothers. Now it is only a short step to finding Adam's address (or gasp) maybe even phone number. Ring Basil six times, only to get V. Poncey sounding ansaphone. Will try again tomorrow. That is, if Tomorrow comes. V. Worried about giant asteroid apparently heading towards Earth. If it links up with the one on the hooter of *moi*, it will probably destroy entire Solar System into bargain.

NB today was **National Poetry Day**, dum-di-dum-di-dee. There was a National poetry comp. which tragickally I did not enter, owing to stuffing details at bottom of skule bag several months ago along with Letters Home Etck. It was won by four kids, three of whom were from the SAME family and went to the SAME skule. This was not a cheat, cos the judges don't know who the entries are from. BUT, sez El Chubb, most fascinating true Fact is: they come from a skule which teaches MEDITATION. El Chubb has always argued (see previous bukes) that meditation wld be good for curing werld's evilles and making poets of us all. So there. Think this qualifies as **Interesting new Fact.**

Fri Oct 9
Film Course, 7.30.

7.10 am. Spotz better. Feel V. Nervous re course. Realize have been fancying Alfonso Bertorelli (MUST find out his name, is it Rosselini or Bertorelli, or am I thinking of Ice-cream?) ever since realizing he is most clever and fascinating lekturer I have ever heard.

It is not Lurve, of course, but a desire to Impress him, that overwhelms *moi*. Check portfolio carefully: storyboard, pix of tube, pix of G. Chubb. Notes re soundtrack to show benevolent old bloke as raging wino Etck. Obviously, this is how Real Documentary-makers work, hence famous Lie-on-the-Wall style. Am beginning to realize that if Real Life was as bad as TV makes it luke, we wld all have committed suicide by now. Soaps are there to make you feel your own home life isn't quite so bad after all . . .

11.30 pm. V. Embarrassed to admit what follows, but might as well take you through it, dear fellow Teenage Worriers, just as it happened to *moi*.

This time was determined to leave loads of time for Bus, tube and Acts of God. So, after failing to reach Basil five more times, left early, arrived at tube in no time but remembered New Resolution to Give to Poor, so nobly threw ten p to busker still playing *My Way*, found correct platform and arrived at destination at 7.22.

Confidently wafted through emerald glass doors to be dazzled by blaze of light. All was dark, shadowy and mysterious last time, you may recall, but now Alfonso Bertollini had clearly decided to cut the dramatique licence and get down to bizniss so magnificent display of cameras, lights Etck now clearly visible. Also figure of what must be Essoldo Bastardo (what *is* his name?) sitting at table with his back to me. El Chubb first there for once, so went nervously nearer, to be first to catch pearls dropped from lips of Holy One.

At which point he turned around. Effect of same caused *moi* to jump out of thin flesh-coloured covering that usually holds body together and gibber . . .

In front of me stood a visione of beauty certainly. But not quite in form I had expected . . .

Possibly the bazzoms were a little too big for perfection and eyes a little too far apart. Legs a trifle on the long side and hair unnaturally shiny. But, if I luked like just a corner of this extraordinary WOMAN, I wld not complain.

'Aaaaaaaah. Sorree to scare you,' she purred in that familiar husky voice. 'You are earrrrly. Let me see, was it Lettee?'

'Yeh,' I muttered.

I hadn't really taken in any of my fellow pupils very closely last week, except to note that they were all flash-looking. How could she remember *moi*? I was rather flattered. Also knew that could now throw heart and soul into recapturing heart and soul of Adam and, um, concentrating on Art.

'Well, Lettee,' continued the visione, 'it's so nice to see such enthusiasm. Do you want to show me your worrrk?'

'Um,' said *moi*, helplessly. I told her all about what I meant to do and how it had gone wrong but I was sure I could get better pictures next week and how the story would go.

'Verrrry eeeeeeenterrrresting, I think theeee project 'as reeeeeal promeeeese,' she kindly said, cheering me up.

As I cheered up, the room filled up. The Visione then climbed up on to the lecture podium and held forth. Alfonsa Rosselini. Got it at last, right sex and everything. Blushed to roots of wig. In fact, blushed to roots of soul. Why had I assumed she was a 'He'? Because she was a Professor? Shorely not? Of course, lighting had been V. Bad . . . she had been swathed in capes, hankies Etck with 'oreeble cold'. Still . . . Blush, shame.

Was so overwhelmed by my stupidity that I found it V. Hard to concentrate. At same time, I realized that it was Prof Rosselini herself and none other who had just admired my ideas. Feel V.V. Happy.

Happy that:

1) Need not Worry about being in Lurve with Alfonso now I know she is Alfonsa Rosselini.

2) Can concentrate on werk, knowing that am on right track. If I take loads more pix this week and improve storyboard . . . Think I have V. Good chance of being one of six who gets film made . . .

Worried that:

1) *May* need specs, as cld not tell Alfonso was Alfonsa. Also does this mean am not observant enuf to be grate Film Director?

2) Was so surprised that may not have taken enough notes on her Brilliant interlekshual lekture and therefore not do my Storyboard well enough. Arg. A Teenage Worrier's Life is full of Paaaaain.

Sat Oct 10

Ring Hazel V. Early to pour heart out re Alfonsa Rosselini. She larfed like drain.

'Hah! Alfonsa! A gurl! You daftie!'

'Not a gurl, Hazel, a WOMAN,' I retorted, somewhat huffily.

'And you think you can direct films when you can't even tell the difference between gurlz and boyz. Har har.' (*Sounds of spifflicating chortles, but of course this remark hit home.*)

'It was VERY DARK. And . . . and . . . she had a bad COLD . . . and she was covered in hankies and capes and her voice was all husky and . . .'

'Slow down. I was only pulling your leg. Anyway, it's good because it means you won't get another daft crush and stop concentrating.'

'Whaddya mean "another daft crush"?' (I was feeling V. Huffy by now.)

'Come off it, Letty, you think of NOTHING but boyz.'

'Bloody cheek. I'm going to be werld-famous film director.'

'No, no, you know what I *mean*. You've never known what it is to (gulp, sniff) truly lurve someone, like I lurve Mandy.'

'If you'd seen old Alfonsa, you wouldn't give old Mandy a second look, I can tell you.'

'Sometimes, Letty, you're very superficial, you know that? Has it occurred to you that I don't just look at the surface of people?'

'You can bet your life Mandy's looking at the surface of you though, Haze, you gorgeous thing you.'

'Oh, oh, oh, it's all awful.' (Cascade of sobs, mones, grones. This is not like Hazel.)

'Hazel, what's up?'

Poor Hazel is heartbroken. Her True Lurve's parents are moving house to live in Scotland. Arg, grue, glume, Julia-and-Juliet-type betrayal. No longer can they entwine in luxury and stay nights together in Wilde Pashione. If Hazel's parents knew wot staying the night with Mandy was really all about, they'd have thousand fitz, thinks Hazel.

Also, at Hazel's horrible posh skule she has no real frend to confide in and is sure they wld all stick her head down loo if she admitted she was gay. I am sure this is not the case, because I thort Gurlz at these single-sex skules spent most of their time trying to help each other out re absence of Boyz, but who am I to tell her what to do? Maybe all these posh gurlz really are mad.

'Think of the Romantick walks among the haggis . . . fab Highland games and stuff, when you go to stay,' I offer, lamely. She laughs amidst her tears, I think.

Only Mother emerges with cheery mug, asking am I ready yet?

They're always saying things like this. It's meant to catch you out. Ready for what?

To go and buy a new coat of course.

Arg, pluke-contents. Had forgotten this plan that will put spoke through wheel of Shame-In-Our-Midst pix for one more day. Owing to insoluble poverty situation of parents (maybe I shld just photograph *them*, they're a Shame in My Midst), have had existing mouldy old winter coat since my last year at Primary skule, at that time two sizes too big ('Plenty of room for growth,' sed snooty assistant), now only three sizes too small. Luke like belisha beacon in hamster's cardigan in it, and outer coats V. Unkool at Sluggs anyway even in blizzard. So, rather than have to wear it on film course if it snows, might be better to at least be involved in choice of new one. Spirits also lifted slightly at thought of day out with Only Mother – V. Rare to spend any time in her company these daze, and when not confronted with lunatic presence of Adored but Exasperating Father, she can be a diff woman.

But of course we had to take Benjy too and all conversation centred round him, as usual.

Trailed dismally round Bent Dross shopping centre. Only coats were sludge-coloured Michelin man type ones made of shiny nylonette, or V. Posh designer labels available only to squillionaires and V. Fastmoving shoplifters. Despite protestations to Only Mother that Wld Rather Die, Hibernate for Entire Winter, go on Blind Date in binliner, had to get nylonette sludge. I now resemble belisha beacon disguised as yak.

As you know, dear reader, El Chubb is no slave to fashion's whims, but I do not want to be

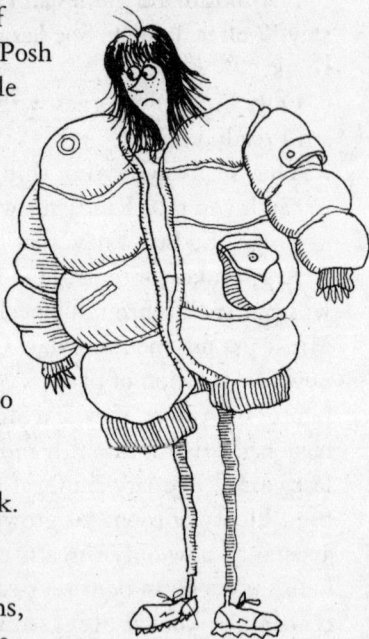

Moi engulfed in nylonette-coat-of-glume

seen dead or alive in this horrific item. Spend journey home wondering if skule bag is big enough to accommodate it squashed up . . .

Home. V. Tired.

Spent remaining four hours of day at desk.

'D'you realize,' I guiltily hear the proud tones of Father, 'Letty's been doing her homework in her bedroom up there for four hours.'

But I was writing to Adam. And this is what I wrote:

Darling Adam,

I can no longer bear to hide my love for you. I have thought of nothing but you since I first caught sight of your blackberry curls and winsome limbs as we suffered under the philistine yoke of Hollywood values (which I am sure you are fighting courageously against, now you are, tragically, in their midst). Please please please say you will be mine for ever. You know that Daniel Hope meant nothing to me and is the scum of the earth, whereas you and I have twin souls that could fly together and transform the world's cinema as well as singing in undying lurve.

A million kisses
forever Yours,
Letty.

(In case you think this letter is V. Restrained, I shld admit it is the tenth draft and I have crossed out 'dearest, darling, loads of lurve,' and much more embarrassing things to get to this point. I *THINK* it is the kind of letter Adam will like. But of course will never send it.)

Still no answer from Basil. This time, heart in mouth Etck, I dared to leave a message: 'You don't know me, but I'm a friend of Adam Stone's and I wondered if you have his address or phone number?'

Decided to recover from this exhausting experience by Luxuriating in foaming bath and washing wig. Only to find foam bath and shampoo have both been used by Benjy in a potion. Use V. Small amount of washing-up liquid for wig, which turns out to be Bad Thing. Transforms luckless wig from snakes rolled in diesel fule, soy sauce and vinegar to strange candyfloss effect as if plugged into electric socket.

Father home V. Late, smelling of Old Bastard lager and, wait for it, wild flowers and roses. Surely he is not canoodling with someone who can afford £47,000 for a flask of scent?

Sun Oct 11
Succoth, last day.

ARG. Last Day of Succoth. Still haven't found out wot it is, and since pluke still reverberates threateningly at end of hooter, have possibly proved beyond reasonable doubt that it isn't that.

Noon: Sleep through alarm as Benjy invaded rume last night. Said that entire floor had been turned into Bird's Nest Soup by Chinese waiters who were really Secret Agents in James Bond-type action thriller. Only Escape was to eat his way out. Had woken in terror at prospect of prawns on toast.

Will make rigorous list of how best to effect day's werk:

Things to do:
1) Cooking lesson with Granny Chubb.
2) Three hours' homewerk.
3) *Photos.*

Must prioritize photos, obviously. But will drop by Granny Chubb's first just to let her know I'll come next Sun for cooking lesson.

11.30 pm. Heartbroken on arriving at Granny Chubb's at lunchtime to find that she had spent last five p on getting cooking lesson ready, consisting of two eggs, one rasher of bacon and four mushrooms.

Could not possibly say 'no' to this mooooving display.

As it turned out, spent V. Happy hour learning how to fry an egg, bacon and mushrooms 'just right' and how to boil an egg 'just right'.

I let G. Chubb have all the bacon and mushrooms as I know this is a luxury for her. I have my life stretching endlessly before me whereas hers is stretching endlessly behind, and right now I am not altogether sure which is better . . .

We looked at some more of her photos and I begged just one more for my portfolio. I can give it back at next week's lesson (apple pie).

It is, I suddenly realize, a truly amazing picture: Underground shelter in the Blitz. Loads and loads of people squashed together like sardines and luking surprisingly cheerful considering they don't know whether or not a Vast Beumb is going to drop and bury them all. G. Chubb looking V. Pretty in a fetching warden's helmet and clutching my infant father. Shed tear at thought of his once golden curls like Benjy's and think it a pity we have to grow up. G. Chubb V. Stern as I voice this thought.

'Not all those kiddies did grow up,' she says.

V. Moved by this experience, I sally forth once more into the seething bowels of tube and take, I think, the best pix I have ever snapped.

All the poor of London seemed to be gathered in the tubes today. Took loads of pictures. Millions of buskers playing it their way, loads of gurlz not much older than me with toddlers disguised as babies, begging for dosh. If they have to stuff a bottle in the mouth of a five-year-old and stick an old bonnet on it, they deserve all the dosh they can get, sez El Chubb, feeling grateful for my

hovel, family Etck. I think my best picture though
was of a toothless old crone ferreting about under
the tube seat for a crisp packet that still had a crisp
in it.

Fantastic.

Got back V. Late to be confronted by my mother
waving a horrible, slimy, bulbous monster at me.
Wonder if Global Warming has sparked attack of
Giant Man-eating Larvae. Impressed at first by Kule
of Larva-Conquering Only Mother, until realization
it is my new coat.

'I'm not dragging all round Bent Dross spending
a fortune on clothes for you to find you go out in the
freezing cold without them! Do you think I'm made
of money?' Etck. Etck.

I sometimes feel that if my mother had known
she wld be talking like this one day when she was
my age, she wld have walked off cliff, or even Cliff,
since there was a time when against her better
judgement she found the Saintly Knight Of Pop a
bit of all right, as they used to say.

When I have children here are four things I will
never say:

'Money doesn't grow on trees.'
'What do you think I am? A slave?'
'No-one listens to a word I say.'
'What time do you call this?'

I'm sure, dear readers, you have a good long list of
parental clichés of your own. Feel free to send them
to *moi*.

Parental ~~Clichs~~ ~~Clitche~~ Clichés

① You never listen to word I say
② Do you think I'm made of money
③ When I was your age...
④ If you think I'm a brussell sprout you've got another think coming (Ha! Just put that in to check you're reading this).

FILL IN YOUR OWN HERE:

As if to prove her right, I started sneezing immediately and went all pathetick. Usually the only way to get my mother on my side is to have V. Bad Cold. This makes her feel V. Guilty about not being a Good Enuf Mother Etck, and she occasionally even goes so far as to tuck me up with a boiled egg – I'd prefer a hot water-bottle of course, ha ha yeech.

Tonight she said I only had *moi*self to blame, had I done my homework, and there was no point in looking pathetic because there was no hot lemon Hooterhug left. No Hooterhug! Tragedy strikes. If I can't have hot Hooterhug my cold will balloon into full-blown pneumonia and I will miss my film course and die.

Am now snuffling with Rover, hot water-bottle and three hours' undone homewerk. V. Hard to concentrate as Benjy had his best frend, Bugsy, and his little brother Duane round, making potions. Why can't he learn to make Hooterhug and be a Useful Person? Only Mother does not like Bugsy. Sez he comes from dodgy family and nicks biscuits. I nick biscuits if poss. So does Benjy.

After Bugsy and Duane go, we spent two hours rubbing down surfaces to get remains of potion out of carpet. Horrified to see Benjy about to douse my camera with potion remains. Saved in nick of time. The life of a Teenage Worrier is haaaaaard, haaaaaaard, haaaaaard.

Mon Oct 12

Columbus day, USA. Thanksgiving, Canada. Shemini
Atzereth.

Spotz almost gone, except for teeny cluster round
chin. Have lernt **New fact** that Christopher
Columbus, whose day this is, died in poverty.

V. Sad when you think if he had been alive today
he cld have made a fortune doing Travel
programmes on the telly. (On the other hand he wld
not have discovered America, as someone wld prob
have got there by now. And anyway, he didn't really
discover it cos the Indians, I mean Native
Americans, got there first. Life is a Hall of Mirrors,
eh?)

Went to skule with sinking heart. (V.
Disappointed to find cold not turned into
pneumonia so must find another excuse for having
failed to do homewerk.) Only ray of hope is, my
photos. Harvey sez he can print them for tomorrow
and I vow to lurve him for ever. Maybe I shld admit
that this is not a GCSE project? But then he
wouldn't do them for me would he? Arg, Guilt,
Shame . . .

Asked Aggy if she has seen Basil as he hasn't
returned my calls. She sed she thinks he's got job
involving travel and will be back next weekend. Am
anguished re letter to Adam. Realize how little I
know about him . . . Decide to pluck up courage
and ring L.A. After V. Diff time with International

80

Enquiries, manage to discover number of Mogul Mogul Junior the Third's film Empire. Tremblingly dial. Receive much longer version of following message: *'Hi. You have been connected to Mogul Movies. If you wish to hear the names of all the movies we have made, including budgets, stars and directors, press 2. If you wish to contact marketing and development press 3. If you wish the direct line of the president in order to tell him personally how stoopid and ignorant his stoopid and ignorant movies are helping to make the population of the Werld, press 4 . . .'*

Well, I made up that last bit, but sometimes I wonder if the people making Hollywood movies have any contact at all with normal Worriers like you and *moi* . . . or they wouldn't seriously talk about their characters in TV interviews as if they had anything at all to do with Real Life. I have mixed feelings about Adam working for such people, though if he swept *moi* away into Tinseltown tomorrow, they wld prob become unmixed qu quickly.

Anyway, the Mogul message continued with: *'If you wish to speak with an operator, please hold.'* I held. I listened to ten minutes of soundtrack from the gratest movies of All Time (all, it seems, made by Mogul). Then came a bouncy apple-pie voice: *'All our operators are either busy or in bed. They have a pretty exciting life outside of Mogul too – that's show business! Office hours are 7.30 am to 9.00 pm, west coast time – please call again. Have a nice night! Don't do anything we wouldn't do! And try not to hurt your fellow human beings doing it!'*

And I thought I had mixed feelings. Anyway, did quick calculation and realized time in Los Angeles was 1 am.

Also did quick calculation of cost of call. Fainted. (Joke.) Realized that telephone operator at Mogul Movies unlikely to know whereabouts of Adam Stone. Left one more message for Basil, heartrendingly begging him to call the minute he returned.

V. Miserable phone call from Hazel.

'Mandy's leaving on Saturday (moan, snuffle, sob). I may never see her ever again.' (boooooo, hooooo)

'Course you will, Haze. You'll be in and out of Castles . . . having stag parties . . .'

'Gawd. You're just like all the rest. Mention Scotland and everyone goes "och aye the noo".'

'Oh, well they probably haven't seen that authentic old Scottish Australian Hollywood history movie, *Braveheart* . . .'

On cheerier note, Mother seems V. Skittish and sez Adored Father on verge of V. Good buke deal (she thinks). Apparently he has shown V. Slim slither of his new novel to agent, who sez this cld be the one to Finally Crack bestseller lists, film rights, Buker Prize for bukes and so on.

This V.V. Good news, since as far as I can see all Adored Father has done in last two years is to play GOD on computer. Still, if a few pages can convince

Mr Alibi at Global Shark Agency to cough up a few measly quid who am I to complain? Take news with pinch of salt however as V. Wonderful Things of this kind have so often lit up spirits of my Adored Family, only to crumble into dust.

Also, the agent wants to see a thing called a 'synopsis', which I thought at first meant a list of all the Naughty Bitz people in the buke do with each other, but turns out to mean a kind of layout of the plot like my film storyboard. Father can't lay his hands on it right now, but sez it's 'somewhere in his study'. That means it cld take years to find, or poss for ever.

Still, Father bouncily bounces in with Fish and Chips for all (he thinks this is the height of champagne socialism if he really goes mad and visits the posh chippie where it costs twice as much and they have pix on the walls of celebs eating their chips out of upmarket newspapers).

'You've got a face like a wet Wednesday,' he cheerily jibes. 'Enjoy the moment, anticipation is the better part of valour.' He may be right, for once. It is better to look forward to a Wonderful Thing – so even if it doesn't happen, you have still had joy of looking forward Etck. (Also have misery of Bitter Disappointment. There is a lot to lern in Life.)

However, much cheered by rare atmosphere of Adored Family in Good Spirits. Parents announce dinner with Alibi on Wed. Big Moment in Chubb PLC future. Agree, in rash moment (and for small

amount of dosh) to babysit every Wed until
Christmas.

'Your father and I need to be alone together
sometimes, darling,' says Mother, flashing Adored
Father face like Sharon Grone, well nearly. Benjy
flashes all of us face like ailing haddock. He *hates* it
when they go out.

11 pm. Have had V. Boring evening doing Maths
revision sheets. Rover traumatized and sits on my
Hed while I struggle with eville mathes. Then, as if
to confirm twilight of glume, Brian Bolt rings
asking me to *Saving Private Ryan*. He certainly
knows how to thrill a Gurl, though maybe he thinks
shotz of young men vomiting, crying, searching for
Missing Bitz Etck will make him luke better than
he usually does, and that in Terror of Moment I will
bury self in his manly Bod.

Should go, I spose, specially as have now decided
that my film will be gratest anti-war (as well a anti-
poverty) movie in history. But have V. Bad feeling
that I may throw up or hide under seat, jumping out
of skin every time somebody treads on a popcorn.
Also, do not want to raise Brian's hopes re nooky.
Grone. Will think about it tomorrow.

Get my photos tomorrow. Can't wait.

Tue Oct 13
Simchath Torah

Rushed into skule V. Early this morning, which left
no time for teeth cleaning (bad) or spot examining
(good).

But Harvey was not in.

Darkrume was locked and bolted. Not surprising,
really. Last time it was left unattended, everything
was nicked. Mr Portillo threatened to close Dept,
sent fierce letter to parents re Marvellous Facilities
wasted on krap pupils with No Respect Etck. Pubic,
sorry, public-spirited El Chubb got petition up to
persuade him to chance it for one more term.

Raced back at lunchtime, still dreading locked
door. No Harvey. Go to nice secretary, Mrs
Dumpling (Mrs Hornet, glad to say, was off sick,
possibly with self-inflicted wound). Harvey's in
hospital. She doesn't know when he'll be back. Sez
much as she wld like to, more than her job's worth
to give me the keys.

Still have two more days till the course, but
thingz not luking good. Staggered through eville
mathes and freezing PE. Hit six times on knuckles,
three times on ankles and once on knee by hockey
sticks. If I go to see *Private Ryan* they'll prob think
I'm one of the cast and let me in for nothing.

Now, cannot concentrate or sleep. Have horrible
visiones of Harvey mutilated under bus, and not yet
done my photos. Or done them but darkrume is

locked for a week as Mark of Respect? Imagine pleading with shocked and disapproving Mrs Hornet ('This of all times is not the moment to be thinking only of yourself, Leticia'), trying to perswade her that Survival of Art is what Harvey wld have wanted.

Aaaaarg. Must sleep, will try to imagine self in soothing embrace of Adam . . . Rover does her best to oblige, but sadly, no contest . . .

Wed Oct 14
Babysit

7 am. Attempted to find blissful sleep last night in imaginary arms of Adam. Kept finding Ghastly Candice Carthage wriggling between us in only gold calf-skin boots and a thong. This distracted Adam, can't think why.

Finally drifted off about 2 am . . . And now, a quick luke in mirror reveals Halloween eyes, spots like erupting volcanoes, strange puffy patches poss indicating terminal skin disorder.

Who cares? sez attempt at new relaxed El Chubb attitude. You don't need looks to be a movie director, look at Q. Tarantino and W. Allen . . . Just as well, cos either my nose has grown in night, or else someone has lopped two centimetres off my tape measure.

11.30 pm. Bliss bliss bliss. Unadulterated bliss. Harvey isn't dead. (NB **New Werd:** have always thought **unadulterated** must mean someone who is not yet an adult or someone who has not committed adultery. But it means, dear fellow Teenage Worriers in the vineyards of glume, *pure*. I know that sometimes there doesn't seem to be much in the Werld you can attach this werd to, but I wld certainly attach it to Granny Chubb frinstance. Not Benjy, despite extreme Yoof.)

'Harvey,' I cried, flinging myself upon his spindly octogenarian form with flailing pashione. 'You're alive!'

'That's a relief,' he replied. I somehow feel he knew that my photos, rather than his survival, were uppermost in my mind. It turned out he had simply gone to have an ingrowing toenail removed. Anyway, he hobbled off to find my contact sheets. Did I say unadulterated bliss? Not exactly. Sight of pix changed all that. Pix of old crone scoffing last crisp Etck looked more like someone's V. Friendly Granny happily tucking in. Pix of beggar women with scruffy toddlers dressed up as babies seem to have come out luking exactly like the V. Worried, financially unchallenged middle-class mums at St Aubergine's, Benjy's old playgroup, which just goes to show:

a) thingz can luke different in life to on camera,

2) there is more to photography than remembering to put the film in, and

c) Worry is def. not good for lines on the mug even if you can afford the odd truckload of non-animal-tested slap.

However, by grate gude luck – and this is where the bliss bit comes in – there were three or four really fantastic pictures of two tiny kidz asleep under piles of old newspapers. One just had its little hands and a tuft of stringy hair sticking out pathetickally. The other's face was covered in snot and grime. They were like something out of *Oliver!*

'Tsk,' muttered Harvey. 'Fancy little kids like that sleeping out. What did we fight the War for?'

Cut short fascinating and humbling conv. with Harvey about our ancestors' struggle on our behalf against the evil fascists to beg him on bended knee to print up the best four pix. Felt wave of guilt when he said how nice it was to see someone working so hard at their GCSEs, but waved it away when thought how the money from my film wld buy glasses for Granny Chubb. Swore to *moi*self to give some to V. Good war veterans charity also after having bought sports car, heli-pad, jet skis Etck. Isn't it weird that the stuff you think is good often turns out rubbish and the stuff you don't notice can often be your best werk? I couldn't even remember taking the pix of the little kids, but they must have been in that bunch of homeless people outside the tube station. Wot a stroke of luck.

Had to babysit so parents could go out on town and attempt to squeeze bludde out of stone in form of massive amounts of dosh from agent on Father's 'novel'. So I put Benjy in front of video and spent all evening arranging portfolio, leaving space for the four new pix that will be ready tomorrow.

This storyboard thing's not as easy as it sounds

Have decided that as camera pans over pix of Kidz in rubbish, there will be a delicately ironic theme tune or maybe a nursery rhyme? If budget runs to it, can intercut these tragick pix of contemporary despair with posh Kidz sitting on rocking-horses in Chelsea, eating boiled egge with silver spunes . . .

Realized to my Horror that video not a PG as had thought, but a 15. Benjy making bludde-curdling machine-gun noises that are not soothed by *Fluff the Magic Puppy*. Insists on sleeping in my room with all the lights on. Carry him to his own bed when fast asleep. Parents still not in and it is nearly midnight. Will Not Worry that they have been run over, but will soothe self to sleep to strains of Eagle Eye Cherry. Sigh.

Thurs Oct 15

Basil rang. He has BEEN in L.A. And SEEN Adam!
I am reduced to nervous wreck at thought of my
belurved still walking and talking on planet Earth.
It has been soooo looong since I have seen his
winsome limbs, blackberry curls, heard his sonorous
tones . . . I could not bring self to ask Basil anything
personal. Too shy. Tried to sound as casual as
someone who has left six messages in one day can
sound. After all, I don't know Basil from, er, Adam.
In my best mock laid-back voice I asked, 'Er, might
it be possible, to um, phone Adam? No big deal,
you know, just a chat.'

'Not easy. He's never in one place for long, and
the time difference makes it harder. Why not e-mail
him?'

Other Teenage Worriers have thrusting,
successful parents like Hazel's, with e-mail, satellite
telly, cable stations, flat-screen TV, mix 'n' match
mobile phones, BMWs, computers that talk,
doorhandles that stay on. Not *moi*. But what I said
was, 'Oh. Great.' And wrote down Adam's e-mail
address. Maybe Hazel wld let me have a go on her
dad's e-mail . . .

'Anyway, he'll be back soon.'

Thud. Thud. That herd of wildebeest galloping
over my vital organs again. 'Yssskpl? Mrrrrph.'

'Eh? You all right?'

'Splllfffft.'

'Whossermatter?' asked the bemused Basil.

'N-nothing. M-ssssffflkghtpppppppffff . . . must be the ph-ph-ph-phone.'

'OK. See ya.'

'Wait!'

'Huh?'

'Only, did you j-j-j-just say Ad-d-d-ddddd-d-dDAMN! Would be back soon?'

'Sure, in a month or so. I'll let you know the flight if you like. Are you sure you're OK?'

'Oh. Sure. Thanks. No problem.'

'OK. See ya.'

'See ya.'

Adam was coming back. Back to London. Back, surely, to *moi* . . . (AND I did manage also to get real address of real house Adam is akshully staying at, which was a relief. Sometimes you think people with cyberspace addresses have been turned from Yuman Beans into strings of computer code and are living in a silicon chip nobody knows where.)

A month. A little, short, tiny, achingly looooooong month. Spent whole evening rewriting letter to Adam eight times, trying to get tone just right, explaining about how I lurved him alone (but not too much) and how Daniel Hope now meant nothing to me any more. Also casually mentioned film course and serious ambitions so as not to sound too weedy.

Final version made me V. Proud akshully. Qu. low-key with only two kisses at end, and written in sensible blue pen on cream paper instead of nauseating pink with hearts on (I blush to think of them and hope against hope he never did see them).

Finally, addressed envelope. Licked it. Closed it. Opened it. Rewrote it twice more. Here is the final version:

Dear Adam,

I just want to explain that this is the seventh letter I have written but I don't think you ever saw the others. If you sent them back unopened, you will do the same with this one and won't be reading it anyway. BUT, if this one does get opened by you, all I can do is explain.

Yes . . . I did arrange to see Daniel Hope in a moment of madness. But no, NOTHING happened between us, nor ever will.

Since you went, I have been occupying myself by making a deeply serious film about War and poverty, which I am hoping will appeal to all nations and classes and – who knows? – perhaps make a small difference to the uncaring world we inhabit. I intend to send copies to President of the USA and the Prime Minister for starters and would so love to hear your opinion of it. Because, I must admit, that though my work is of great importance to me, you are the person I think of all the time. If you ever think of me, please write. Basil tells me you are coming home soon . . . ?

Yours,

Letty. x x.

Found new envelope. Put on stamp. Then, before
I had time to Worry more, raced down road and,
YES, posted it. The minute the letter had left my
hand I was filled with doubts and regrets. Was it
self-important? Too affectionate? Would one kiss
have luked kuler than two? Decided no kisses wld
be better so hovered glumily round post box waiting
for postperson so I cld retrieve letter. Then realized
there was no collection till 8.30 am. Which wld be
when I was on my way to skule. The fates had
decided. I wld leave it.

I feel much better having done this. The weight
of Adam thinking I had betrayed him has rested
heavy on my heart. If he lurves another now, so be
it. At least I have bared a zillionth of my soul to him
and tried to explain myself.

Harvey has done my photos brilliantly. Spent all
evening sticking them in portfolio alongside V.
Moving story plus suggestions about sound effects. I
think the muffled cries of infants, wailing sirens and
bombs will do for starters. Cannot decide whether
Humpty Dumpty or *Twinkle, Twinkle, Little Star* wld
be most appropriate nursery rhyme. Need feeling of
deep irony as charming tune counterpoised with
horrific pix Etck to pull at viewers' heartstrings . . .
Otherwise, V. Pleased with results.

Grue. Remember that in a weak moment I said
yes to Brian Bolt and am therefore going to *Saving
Private Ryan* on Sat. Maybe I can wear shades so that

no-one will notice if I close my eyes, poss conceal sick bag inside layers of Coat-Of-Glume, which I will wear to put him off.

Fri Oct 16
Film Course, 7.30

Midnight. I can't believe what happened today.

Had nightmare journey to film course on most crowded tube in universe, crammed between mass of surging bods and unable to hang on to vast portfolio beneath stampede of football hooligans chanting 'Yor Bad and you knooow you are, yor Mad and you knooow you are.' Had to virtually garrotte old lady in order to retrieve crushed life's werk. Maybe I shld make film about hopeless Teenage Worriers slaughtering ancient generation to make tubes into Places of Safety?

Arrived on time, feeling V. Nervous. I was about eighth in line to show my work and was feeling V. Twitchy as everyone in front of me looked so flash, clever Etck, and had portfolios the size of cupboards, bulging with stuff. Also, they all have access to home video cameras and seem to have been on zillions of other courses, squawking on about *'texts'* and *'representation'* and *'rhetoric'* and *'agenda'* and stuff. It felt just like when you hand in a project at skule which you have knocked off in about ten minutes on lined paper with biro, and the gurl in front is producing a twenty-page handbound buke with gold lettering on the cover all typed out on her dad's posh computer (and prob typed out by her dad, too . . .)

BUT, as they showed their work, my confidence rose . . .

Kurt Flasher unrolled a script roughly ninety pages long about British waterways (??**!!) and droned on for ten minutes explaining the opening shot. Alfonsa Rosselini, somewhat tersely, pointed out that we were making three-minute 'shorts'. Kurt retired under cloud.

Veronica Saffron-Walden had developed a short story about an urchin from an estate with voice like Whitney Houston, who is thus discovered by a millionaire producer and catapulted to fame.

'Who weeell play theeeee girrrl?' questioned Alfonsa Rosselini in her voluptuous rolling Italian tones.

'Well, me, I thought,' blushed Veronica, who looked as much like an urchin as Pavarotti looks like a jockey.

'And can you seeeeeeeng?'

'I was thinking of taking lessons.'

Bageshott Hardy's Mystery-murder-whodunnit unravelled as he hadn't worked out whodunnit yet but thought it might emerge 'through the process'.

And so it went on.

Alfonsa Rosselini began to look at her watch and tap her foot. In little hesitant flutters, the diminutive confidence of El Chubb began to stir.

When my turn came, it had grown so fast that I opened my briefcase with a triumphant flourish usually foreign to any movement of *moi*self in public, apart from running in the other direction.

And out fell . . .

. . . an assortment of very dodgy-looking ladies' underwear, wigs, suspenders, high heels and fishnet tights.

'I don't want to deeeeescourage you,' said Alfonsa Rosselini, her arctic tone quelling the surrounding sniggers, 'but don't you theenk there are quite enough of thees kind of movies already?'

Horror. I must have picked up the WRONG briefcase as I struggled off the tube. I stood, burning in flames of hell, gazing dumbly at the billowing folds of a ballgown covered in little sprigs of violet that was still snaking out of my briefcase. Alfonsa turned to clever Clementine.

I could hear Alfonsa Rosselini as if in some dim echo chamber beginning to choose the six best projects. I knew now there was no hope for mine. Unable to speak, I stumbled out into the night, clutching the briefcase-of-horror grimly, tears lashing my windswept mug.

I have V. Little memory of my journey home . . .

Any hopes of comfort in the bosom of my family were savaged by ballistic Father who was roaring, as I returned, about the synopsis of his novel, which was still missing and was now a matter of urgency.

'*Surely* you saved?' screamed Only Screaming Mother.

'NO! Oh, God!' screamed Adored Louder Screaming Father. 'I was just about to press *save* when the computer froze. I'd only printed out the one copy . . .'

'If your apology for an office was less like a war zone maybe you could find it.' Bang, slam, crash.

I slunk off to my lonely rume, alone with my pain and a briefcase full of stuff that they wouldn't even allow on *Eurotrash*. It's Amazing women dress up in this kind of stuff, must be V. Uncomfortable.

So. Father has lost novel synopsis.

I, meanwhile, have lost life's werk. But does anybody care?

2 am. Woke, fully dressed. Realized I must write to Alfonsa Rosselini to explain what happened. Hope against hope that I had left my name and address in my portfolio. Did I? Did I?

Then realized, in panic, that I hadn't looked inside the one I picked up. Doubtful the owner wld leave a name and number in it. If you lost this stuff there's no knowing who you'd get on the end of the phone. However searched feverishly among scarlet satin underwear, high-heeled shoes, padded bras — and found small business card. *D.F. Springer* and a phone number. Faintest ray of hope dawns that D. Springer has picked up my briefcase. If only, if only . . .

Sat Oct 17

Left message on Miss Springer's ansaphone. Edinburgh number, apparently. Arg. If Davina Springer, or whoever she is, has gone back to Edinburgh with my briefcase, how will I get it back??

Spent the rest of the morning composing letter to Alfonsa Rosselini. Realize I obviously won't have the courage to go back . . . but still I felt deep urge, yearning need, to express self.

Then at 6.30, just as I was settling down for an evening of brane-numbing TV, horror of horrors *Brian* turns up, dressed like dog's dinner in full designer rig, flashing labels on every pocket. *Moi* only in old sack Etck as I had completely forgotten our date. Still, at least the fact that I had not even washed face or dragged comb through wig will have shown him wot I feel for him: zero.

To my massive relief, queues for *Private Ryan* stretch round block (mostly thirteen-year-old Boyz standing on tiptoe and wearing army jackets) so we went to *The Horse Whisperer* instead. Was Horrified at gore and had to muffle sobs at the sight of the poor wounded animal bleeding on to the snow Etck so if it had been *Private Ryan* wld certainly have had full-scale nervous breakdown. V. Scared that Brian might try to put comforting arm round *moi*. But maybe he has learnt his lesson. Or probably I just luked too repellent, even for him, what with puffy eyes, haggard sleepless mug, old sack (arg, too ugly even for Brian Bolt . . .).

Now realize that if can't take one horse being wounded wot hope is there for *moi* as fearless anti-war campaigner?

Got home (did NOT ask Brian in) to find message written by Benjy on kitchen table saying someone called Bozzle has rung.

Who?

Basil! Oh, Oh! Too late to phone back.

Sun Oct 18

Phoned Bozzle first thing. V. Grumpy at being woken up. Just said he'd heard that Adam coming back 'in ten days or so' and that he wld be throwing a welcome home party for him and wld I like to let a few other old mates know? Would I like to roll in warm fudge? Yes yes yesssss!

Tried, as casually as possible, to find out further details like flight number, exact time of return, whether Adam was eating properly Etck Etck, while wildly thinking I knew no-one else who knew Adam at all and had rung Basil under V. False pretences. But he just politely asked me if I always rang people this early on Sunday morning and he'd like a little more kip if I didn't mind.

The thort that Adam will find out about the briefcase-of-horror and my complete failure as artiste weighed heavily on my soul. So much for influencing world leaders with my grate werk. Dragged self round to cooking lesson with Granny Chubb (apple pie).

First thing she asks for is her photos back. I hadn't even thought of how she wld feel about them . . .

'S-sorry,' I muttered. 'Meant to bring them. Forgot. Really sorry.' Looked at her ashen face. Oh God, she probably sleeps with that one of her and my infant father under her pillow. Maybe she kisses it at night? WHY oh WHY didn't I get them copied? It wld have been perfectly easy. Harvey wld have done it for nothing.

Staggered through the cooking lesson, dropping cloves and bits of pastry all over G. Chubb's spotless lino (how does she keep everything so clean when she can hardly see her hands, let alone the stove, in front of her face? How does she avoid third-degree burns?) and gratefully consumed half of burnt apple pie (my fault, turned oven up to gas mark 10, must be unconscious desire to set light to Self like protesting Kurd Etck).

Arrived home to find Basil had phoned again.

'What did he say? Can't anyone in this house ever take a simple message?' (Funny how quickly parental habit of turning any stray bit of Bad News into latest in long line of Utter Catastrophes infects optimistic Younger Generation.)

'That's rich, coming from you,' says sarcastic

Mother, peering at me from over latest canvas.

Stormed from rume in fury, tripping over anguished Rover. Scooped up my poor neglected pet and attempted to stamp on the repellent Kitty's tail in vengeance. Missed and stamped socked foot on strange vehicle bristling with plastic figures in helmets.

'That my War machine,' wailed Benjy. 'That there to KILL the floor.'

Have now got Lacerated Sole to add to Lacerated Soul, raging sore throat and violent headache. Obviously meningitis on way, prob V. Good Thing as will no longer be any trouble to anyone. But who will look after Rover?

Woke about an hour later, sneezing. Pushed Rover off Hed to see Only Mother, holding steaming mug. Was it cocoa or Hooterhug? She drank it in one go and said, 'Someone called something Springer on the phone for you. Sounds very evasive. Says it's about a briefcase. Are you in any kind of trouble?'

Trouble? If only she knew. Stagger out of bed, but Benjy has put the receiver back 'to tidy up'. Only postpone killing him to ring D. Springer's number. Have strange feeling she is called Deirdre. No answer. Can't believe it. She was there only a minute ago!

Throat now feels as if pterodactyls and alligators were partying inside it. Feel too ill to kill Benjy. Anyway, he is upset that his favourite kids TV presenter has been sacked for drugs orgy. Benjy will miss his cheery face. How will they explain it to kiddies? Only Mother has been furious that rude President Clinton stuff was all over papers, but at least Benjy couldn't read it. He heard about the cigar incident though. Luckily thought it was just that people were cross with the president for smoking.

Mon Oct 19
Diwali.

Hmmph. Festival of light. *Moi* **am candle blown out.**

Phoned Deirdre Springer first thing. No luck. Meningitis sadly cured, leaving only gharstly throb. Was able to move toe. Not allowed to stay off skule. Dragged self to glumey Sluggs through driving rain encased in nylonette coat-of-glume. Throat felt like gnarled oak in parched desert. (Thinks: cld you plant an oak in the Yemen?)

David Springer, presumably Deirdre's husband, finally got through this evening, desperate to pick up wife's briefcase. Must be qu. an interesting partnership, briefly think to Self.

David sez he will be in London on Wed and MUST have it then. AND, yesssssss . . . he has my

own briefcase safe and sound. Arrange to meet him for swap in caff near Sluggs after skule. Hope nobody I know is in there. Might be awkward questions. Maybe OK if Dodgy Briefcase doesn't burst open. Babysitting night, but shld be back in plenty of time.

Huge relief. Feel almost happy for first time in LIFE, so it seems. At least I will be able to return Granny Chubb's pix, even if my career as film-maker and winner of thousand spondoogle prize is now beyond reach.

Tue Oct 20

Grate joy of knowing my photos will soon be back in my greasy paws made me full of Milk of Yuman Kindness for a change. V. Sympathetick frinstance to weeping Priscilla Crump, who appears not to have handed in any homewerk all term and is V. Emotional.

Realize she is looking somewhat lumpy, but don't like to ask her if she is up the duff. She looked so mournfully at me that I offered her my last piece of fudge and a tissue. Must say sight of her blotchy mug and matted wig makes one realize that there is always somebody Werse Off than oneself. V. Good Lesson for Life. She was just about to Unburden her Soul to me, I feared, when the bell went . . . but not before she had time to reveal that she has detention tomorrow for her homewerk failures, which reminds *moi* that so have I. Aaargh. Yeech. Bleaarh. Life of El Chubb much werse than moony old Priscilla's, having failed to hand in three weeks' homewerk (including, nachurally, the lovelorn sweetheart's letter from World War 1, which went out of my Hed as soon as I had invented it. That, as my old primary teacher Ms Scales wld have said, is the trouble with lies. They always find you out. It is easy to remember the truth, but V. Hard to remember wot you have made up).

Wed Oct 21
Babysit

Detention, of course, goes on way past rendezvous time in caff with *'Undies Fiend Made My Life Laundrette Hell'* maniac, so rushed to appointed place. V. Late. Horrified to see only people there are Syd Snoggs's gang, and a V. Classy-looking woman (well, V. Classy for Cholesterol Charlie's caff) reading a mag. Can't face Snoggs and co, so hung about on street corner in sleet storm for 40 mins waiting.

Was so wet that I was even forced to take nylonette coat-of-glume out of bag and drape it round self. Just as I was about to give up, the woman came out carrying *my* briefcase.

Wot a fule! Why hadn't I thought of it?

Obviously David couldn't make it so he sent *Deirdre*. Carrying my precious briefcase!

But no.

This WAS David. His booming voice made that perfectly clear.

'Thank goodness,' he said. 'It's SO hard to get those shoes in my size and I must have them tonight.'

I gazed down at his enormous feet. He was beautifully dressed in a smart coat and skirt with black nylons with SEAMS up the back and a pair of Doc Martens. I had, actually, noticed that the scarlet high heels in the briefcase-of-horror were V. Big, but just hadn't put two and two together. Also, had to admit that, boots or not, David Springer looked a lot more like a woman than the belisha beacon dressed as mammoth he was talking to.

David and I, now feeling like the best of pals, giggled as we checked the contents of our respective briefcases, sheltering under his vast umbrella. We vowed undying gratitude to each other just as my mad father stormed towards Sluggs, luking for me as I was late to babysit. I attempted to duck behind David's towering form, but the eagle eye of Dad honed in upon me. He exchanged frosty remarks with David and quizzed me fiercely. Got home thanking God Snoggs and co did not spot *moi*. When moaning parents went out I left six messages for Basil, saying all I want is Adam's flight number, but not to worry, it isn't that important . . . Went through portfolio lovingly, thinking I might dare to give film course one last go and hoping against hope that Alfonsa Rosselini had got my letter and understood.

Had cosy evening with Benjy in front of TV and read him *Murder at Monster Mansion* in hope it wld give him fewer nightmares than *Fluff the Magic Puppy*.

Thurs Oct 22

Lots of stuff in paper this morning about how to get 'perfect baby'. Wonder if Shakespeare's mum read it? Pretty soon you'll be able to select the ideal sperm, eggs Etck from mail-order catalogue of eye colours, future bazoom sizes Etck and keep them in the fridge for the appropriate moment. Not sure I like the idea of poss future bliss with Adam amounting to us sitting up in bed shaking a test tube and then going 'Was it good for you?' afterwards. However, can't help hoping they'll invent a gene that redistributes bitz of noze to bazzoms, thereby rendering former smaller and latter larger.

Anyway, we Teenage Worriers have more important Worries than how to get a perfect baby – how *not* to have a baby is more pressing as teen pregnancies zooom. Come to think of it, Priscilla Crump has been off sick for a week . . .

EL Chubb's
PERFECT BABY
Toilet trained at birth
No tear ducts ←
Always smiling.
Sez: "I LUV 'OO"
(Puke...bleurghh
If you think THIS
is bad, phone a
scientist).

NB We need tear ducts to
lubricate our luscious peepers.

Fri Oct 23
Film Course, 7.30

Off early from skule. Half term. Yippee!

BRILLIANT evening at film course. Best day of
whole life so far. Alfonsa Rosselini was ECSTATIC
about 'Ze amaaazeeng peex of ze Rubbish Keedies'.
(Hope she doesn't say this when I get on *Thees Ees
Your Life* one day.)

'Thees say so much about the paarlous state of
your nation today,' she continued. (NB **New Werd**.
Parlous meaning extreme, dangerous, difficult to
deal with. Hmmm.) The wonderful Alfonsa then
took me to one side, her vast orbs (eyes, you fule)
overflowing with tenderness. 'Letteee,' she hummed
in her sonorous interlekshual tones, 'you have trooo

understanding and compassion in your soul. Your letter to mee was lovely and the work of a trooo artiste. And we are een luck. Bradley has broken hees neck. So there ees a place for one more project. And eet weel be yoursss.'

Overflowing with joy, I thanked Bradley mentally a thousand times for breaking his neck, threw myself into the course, helping everyone else like mad with their stuff. I've been assigned four people to work on mine with me: V. Nice Australian gurl (who reminds me of Spiggy, unfortunately) called Dot, Kurt (furious his project wasn't chosen), clever Clementine and Stanley, a very quiet round person who hasn't spoken yet. Casually ask Dot how long post takes to get to Oz (thinking, fiendishly, must be about the same time as to Los Angeles). She said it might take five daze to get there and five daze to get reply. Sent letter on 16th, so shld hear, latest, on Mon 26th, the day we go to Sad-on-Sea for Family Holiday.

Home to find no letter, Father snoring in front of *MunnyGrubbers*, floor strewn with cans of Old Bastard lager.

Ponder rare moment of justice for *moi*, tempered only by thought of justice for poor Bradley, now presumably with vast plaster collar keeping his head on like on cheery *Casualty* episodes. Hope his neck not being comfortably supported by lying prone in coffin. Grue, misery, susperstition, I-am-not-werthy.

Sat Oct 24
United Nations Day

United Nations Day. And *moi* at peace with werld, overflowing with milk of yuman kindness, lurve, joy Etck despite no Letter. Disconcerted to see Father at doormat before *moi* and furtively pocketing bright pink envelope . . .

Have decided to practise wot I preach and be V. Kind ray of sunshine to everyone. Am particularly trying to be nice to my poor old father, as now understand wot it's like to lose life's werk. Also, still niggling Worry about whether his glume might turn into depression, forcing him to experience mid-life crisis and abandon Only Family.

Only Mother sez that for blokes of his age it seems to have become *de rigueur* (NB Fancy French phrase for 'the fashion') to trade in their wives for younger, smarter models, rather like cars. They also trade in their Teenage Worriers for younger models and end up being unable to support two families, mone grone. But maybe a few days in Sad-on-Sea will help . . . Not sure that five days in Sad-on-Sea is wot I had in mind for a holiday, but we never go away as family so why not? Only wish Ashley cld come, but some posh bloke at Oxford invited him ski-ing. Also Gharstly to think Adam's letter might arrive while I am away but wonderful to imagine it waiting for me.

However, I digress from general feeling of glee.

I spent whole afternoon with Benjy. Went to park, swang on swings or swinged on swongs, waded through dog poo and then sat by roaring one-bar electric fire and made up New Werds together. Benjy came up with:

Flurg (for stuff in bottom of your pockets)

Skangdoogle (for weird objects you find in drawers but don't know what they are)

Skank (anything nasty)

Ploomp (anything soft)

So exhausted by all this fresh air and interlekshual effort that didn't get round to going through vast box in bedrume to tidy rume properly. Will do tomorrow.

Sun Oct 25

British Summer Time ends
PUT CLOCKS BACK.

Ah, me. One person's happiness is another's glume . . .

Hazel rang early in floods of tears, weeping and wailing about the End of Summer and the departure of her One True Lurve. Felt pang of guilt as had forgotten Mandy was leaving yesterday, but so caught up in own buoyant mood of artistick and lurve hopes that can't think of wot to say to poor old Haze.

Went V. Happily to Granny Chubb. Begged her

to let me keep her pix, which she was touchingly excited to see again, for one more week as have to show them to tutor (did not have heart to tell her they had temporarily been in clutches of large man in frock).

We made Cauliflower Cheese today which was one of best things I have ever tasted. She showed me how to do a roo, which is a sauce where you melt butter, add a little flour, thicken it slowly and then add liquid. G. Chubb says this is qu. normal cooking technique, not something only known to blokes in tall white hats with *Eurotrash* accents. Apparently people make gravy like this, but not my Only Mother whose chicken gravy, lurvingly made once a year, tastes like contents of hot water-bottle with bits of onion in it. **NB New Werd newsflash:** Er, *roo* is akshully French werd: '*roux*', as I was embarrassed to discover later on . . .

On way home, had sudden, blinding-flash feeling it was time to try e-mailing Adam. This involved visit to Hazel, in Mission Impossible attempt to get access to her dad's computer.

Going round to Hazel's always makes *moi* ponder on wealth, poverty, meaning-of-Life. Hazel's house is vastest house in werld, with about five floors, each of them bigger than our entire hovel and makes Buck House look like Horace's cage Etck. The walls are shades of vanilla and magnolia, the carpets ruby red or palest hint-of-cream and so thick you need a machete to cut yr way through.

MIND THE GAP: Although manners may change, the gap between rich and poor, tragickally, is WIDENING

The central heating is always full on so it feels like those tropical plant places in Kew Gdns, and there are mirrors everywhere, which makes *moi* feel dizzy like being in fairground. The effect, though, is far from cosy, as it doesn't feel lived in. This is due to tragick modern Fact of Life that Hazel's folks are always OUT, earning vast amounts of dosh to pay for central heating, Hazel's pony, music lessons and posh skule fees to keep her away from Boyz, the Evil-Sex-Machines-From-Hell, her mother thinks – though it has to be said even V. Docile, stamp-collecting Boyz seem to find it hard to keep their minds on higher things when Hazel appears, but easy to keep their hands on lower things instead, aaargh, shock-horror, yeeech.

Hazel's mum let me in, wearing her usual slightly frantic smile and glancing at my boots to make sure I took them off. 'Letty! Good! Perhaps you can cheer Hazel up,' she said grimly, in the voice of a Teenage Worrier's parent who is at end of tether. Today, the End of British Summertime, was a particularly glumey one for Hazel. I was guided to her rume by intrepid squad of trackers armed with maps, satellite navigation systems and dog-teams (I jest, arf arf, but even though I've been visiting Hazel's house since I was two I still have trouble finding my way around it) and also by her sobs, and spent the next hour wringing out tissues and gazing at photos of Mandy.

I did my best to admire them. I thought Mandy luked a V. Nice, jolly, ordinary sort of Gurl, but then we can't all be goddesses like Hazel, as I told her.

'She's a goddess to me,' cried Hazel, weeping even more copiously, her tears shooting out at right angles like machine-gun fire. Sometimes I think I don't always have the knack of Saying The Right Thing. Cld not think of way to cheer her up, so lamely suggested we go Trick or Treating next Sat. A ghost of a smile hovered round her cupid's bow mouth as we recalled the many Trick-or-Treats we had indulged in over our long years of friendship, taking Innocent Pleasures of Yoof to borders of criminal offences, and leaving zillions of furious neighbours covered in glue, goo, silly string, champing at the bit to come and complain to our Adored Parents, if only they could open front doors firmly tied to next door neighbour's front door by clothesline.

I seized this bonding moment to ask Hazel if I cld borrow her father's computer, just for five minutes, to send a vital e-mail re my film course.

She asked me in V. Surprised voice if it cld really be true my Adored Writer Father didn't have e-mail himself, but I told her he took a long time to catch up with these things, and thought letters still went by Pony Express. Hazel ushered me along several miles of corridor into an office the size of the Albert Hall. With her help setting it up, and with some difficulty preventing her from seeing the True Nature of my message, I sent (I think) this message

115

to Adam: *Letters don't reach you. Will this? Please ring me. Letty.* Very restrained, I think you'll admit, dear reader. I even remembered to put my phone number on it and hoped Adam wld call rather than e-mail Hazel's dad's address, which might turn out a bit embarrassing.

When I got back, was too knackered, wot with consoling and e-mailing, to approach vast Box, except for brief search for socks.

'Hope you've packed,' said Only Mother grimly as I surged into the tender arms of slumber. 'We're leaving at 9.30 sharp.'

Mon Oct 26

Kept checking post despite knowing I wldn't get a letter back from an e-mail sent only yesterday, but Adored Father has taken to grabbing post from mitt of *moi* and scrabbling through it himself. This morning he pocketed another pink envelope surreptitiously before chucking the bills in the bin as usual, humming rather oddly as he did this. Hope mid-life crisis not descending in form of madness. As usual, when family going away, V.V. Bad-tempered packing ensued. Viz:

'Why is it only, EVER, ME that does ANYTHING in this apology for a home?'

'No, Benjy, you can't take your wombat. It won't FIT.'

'Must have wombat! Wombat SCARED on 'is own.'

'Well then you'll have to UNpack Elly, Duck, Bogey and Fartles.'

'MUST have Elly Duck Bogey and Fartles.'

And on. And on.

At 11 am Adored Father remembered several vital phone calls and Only Mother was still writing notes to milkman.

V. Sad to abandon Rover for three days, but she does like staying at Granny Chubb's and at least Granny Chubb is nicer to her than to the horrible Kitty, who everyone else makes such a fuss of just cos she's fluffy and cuddly and not old and flea-bitten. I s'pose our respective pets are a bit like me (manky) and Benjy (cute).

11.30. We are sitting twiddling our thumbs as Father drones on and on on phone to agent and Mother attempts to stuff wombat into boot, or welly boots into wombat, dunno, lost the plot. Have sudden sad urge to be going on family holiday to Majorca, or Mauritius, or Tenerife, or Cuba, or Iraq – anywhere except Sad-on-Sea.

Just as we were leaving, phone rang for ME. Could it be Adam? Responding to my e-mail?? Already? But no. Hazel, weeping.

'See you Saturday, we're just off,' I ruthlessly said.

It rang again. Aggy. Weeping. 'Just spent a day with Mum.'

'Brilliant!'

'Wooooooooaaoo, noooooooooaaoo! Terrible!' Sob,
gulp.

'Why?'

'She's Happy.'

'What? With the *postman*?'

'Y-yes.'

'Oooh, pooooor, poooor Aggs. Gotta go. See you
Saturday.'

Felt V. glumey for my poor frendz, specially
Aggy, who had been hoping against hope that she
cld persuade her mum to return to the family nest.

Arrive in Sad-on-Sea at 4 pm in dusky drizzle.
Journey usual nightmare – Adored Father twitching
and gibbering at slightest unusual sound from car
(don't know how he distinguishes them from usual
sounds of banging, exploding, hissing, clattering
Etck), Only Mother shouting road directions at him
for turnings we just passed, but Benjy blissfully
happy, as he always is in a car, because he doesn't
count either the car or the road as a floor.

Bracing wet walk along deserted pebbly shore,
listening to wild waves crash and thinking own true
lurve somewhere out beyond the champing foam.

Little house V. Cosy with fire, roses on curtains,
doilies Etck. Kind of richer version of Granny
Chubb. Bed to sound of wild wind dashing waves
against cliffs. Sigh.

Tue Oct 27

Sad-on-Sea. Drizzle. Wind. Soggy fish and chips.
Sleet. Cream tea. Doing nothing. Luverly.
BOOKER PRIZE for bukes on telly. Decide in be-
nice-to-Only-Father and improve-mind campaign to
sit up and watch it with him. He rages at flash
'smart arse' toadies on chat show bit all savaging
other writers' bukes. 'Poncey middle class w**s' was
his conclusion, just like last year.

    Have slept like twig since being here. Sea air,
gentle snores of Benjy beside me. Fascinating to find
he is not scared of the floors in this house. Possibly
cos they are tidy? Must experiment by clearing out
his bedrume. And my own. Yawn.

Wed Oct 28

Sad-on-Sea. Steady Drizzle. We all have colds, but
are curiously happy. Only Mother and Father have
not had single row, but just sit like large turnips in
front of roaring fire, gazing into space. Benjy
playing with his little figures (Dr Dume, Professor
Eville, Secret Agent Sinne). I have started *War and
Peace*. Amazing wot a few daze away from the hurly
burly of the Big Smoke can do. Feel deep
sentimental lurve of homely humble British seaside.
Damp rock, slippery rocks, glumey crabs, grey
pebbles, wind, forlorne tea shoppes and all.

Greetings from Sunny SAD-ON SEA, costa del salt

Sad-pix
SX1222

POST OFFICE
PREFERRED
Printed in
Great Britain

Having a
time here.
Wish you
were lovely.
XX Letty
BENJOX

Ashley Chubb
Christchurch
OXFORD
England
Earth

SAD-ON-SEA   GENERAL VIEW

BEACH & CLIFFS   ROUGH SEAS   PLX3111

Thurs Oct 29

Nothing happened today and I lurved every minute.

Fri Oct 30

John Glenn is back in space aged 77. This gives *moi* hope. Maybe one far-off day sixty odd years from now El Chubb will be orbitting lurvely planet Earth. We can but dream . . .

Woke up V. Glumey at thought of going home. Odd, as had dreaded coming. Am on page ten of *War and Peace* and feel V. Pleased with self. Still Peace so far.

Glume considerably deeepened by arrival home to find NO letter from Adam. And nothing on ansaphone either. Maybe e-mails don't werk? Maybe they too are delivered by adult adulterers more interested in shagging yr best frend's mum than doing an honest daze werk? Only message for *moi* is from Hazel, sounding V. Glumey.

My own Glume even werse on noting Only Father pocketing TWO more PINK envelopes.

What does this mean? My fears re Dolores are resurfacing with a vengeance. It has been raining all day and am surprised how much werse it feels in London. Rain is wetter, colder, greyer, bleaker in Big City than it is even in cold wet grey bleak Sad-on-Sea. V. Mysterious. Ponder notion that ye elements affect mude swings more in urban wastescape than amid Nature's bounty, where compensations for krap weather include ability to see vast expanse of heavens, majestick clouds, noble sheep Etck instead of tiny grey square of sky assaulted by high rises.

Tried to ring Basil three times but phone emits horrible gurgling sound, like walking in Wellington boot with hole in. Father stomped next door to Mrs Scrooge to ring phone company to find that there's water in all the phone lines for miles around (except, obviously, Mrs Scrooge's. She dropped a bill round ten minutes later for 30p 'for use of telephonic arrangements'. If there's a long delay to fix the neighbours' phones she'll be in *Sodoff* magazine soon, showing readers around her lovely new home). They will get an engineer to come the week after next, they say. *Week after next.*

122

'Bloody disgrace,' snarls gentle father. 'This is a working household. We need the phone for urgent business. That's what I told them.'

Only bright spot in dank homecoming was joyful reunion with Rover, who has put on weight under tender care of Granny Chubb. Guilty at sight of faint gleam on her fur and hint of shine in her eye, I vow to ask G. Chubb for some cat's recipes on Sun.

Sat Oct 31

Halloween
Arg. Worry.

Spent morning with Benjy, Bugsy and Duane, carving faces in pumpkins.

Spent afternoon in shops with Hazel and Ags getting Trick or Treat stuff. Have to admit I hate Halloween, gives me collywobbles as I fear eville spirits may come out of tombs Etck and go boo. However, too shy to admit this to living souls and felt I must go along with it to cheer frendz. Also thought it might give me chance to slink into Hazel's for few mins to hurl more plaintive cries into the echoing corridors of cyberspace on her dad's computer. With true El Chubb deviousness, and after trailing round spending hard earned babysitting dosh on loominous fingernails, witchy mask and silly string, I casually suggested we try it all on at Hazel's.

'No fear,' she said. 'The folks are having a Halloween supper where they all sit round and read ghost stories . . . creepy.' Apparently Hazel's folks do this every year. Each guest brings a scary story and a candle. They each read, then blow their candle out until the room's dark. Dread to think what they do after that. Never knew her parents were weirdos, but maybe it's the only way they let their hair down. So we all tramp back to my place and recapture our youth dressing up in binbags. Nachurally, Benjy wants to come with us.

And Bugsy and Duane too. Arg.

We cover them in black eyeliner and fluorescent green face paint and I rip up an old pillowcase and daub lipstick on it to look like bludde. Bugsy thrilled. Benjy wails that he wanted to go as a pumpkin, but there's nothing fat and orange in the house except for wombat, so he has to make do.

By the time we got out of the house the rain was falling in solid sheets so we cld barely see which houses had pumpkins Etck in the windows. The first one we went to had a pumpkin that screamed and cackled when we approached. Benjy turned as white as he could in the darkness, binbag et al.

However, must admit the little ones were V. Good for getting sweeties, as they luked rather fetching in their drenched vampire suits. As usual, it was the block of flats full of old people and single parents that gave us the most sweeties. When we got to the posh streets near the park we went bonkers with the silly string and got one pack of mintoes. But not one single bit of fudge. Have decided there is definitely a Big Gap in the Fudge market. Must make own brand and convert werld to this fab sweet.

Saw some good Halloween outfits looming through the glumey downpour, including V. Scary skellington and a vast witch riding a bicycle with a broomstick attached to the back giving V. Good impression of flying. For some weird reason she reminded me of my briefcase-of-horror frend, David Springer.

Tried three phone boxes while we were out to get hold of Basil. All bust. Surprised not to find postcard offering telephonic services from Mrs Scrooge amongst the massage ads.

V. Touched when we returned home to find Only Mother sweating over stove making pumpkin soup 'to warm you all up'. Although inedible, it was a kind thought – maybe she meant we shld pour it into the bath and jump about in it. And she managed to find us a biscuit each as well. The weather had been perfect for Hazel and Aggs as they cld cry as much as they liked and no-one wld notice. They cheered up slightly as we divided the sweeties in front of the electric fire and then left sobbing, arm in arm, into the wild howling night. Bugsy ate my biscuit.

Sun Nov 1

No Birds no bees no health no ease no leaves on trees
november. Time to check out my resolutions.
Yeeeech.

Update Resolutions

1) Write in this diary every day
YESSSS! Miracle.

2) Clean teeth twice a day
Achieved on 20 daze so far, not bad. All you kidz
out there with more than one loo, you don't know
how lucky you are.

**3) Limit spot, zit and pluke examinations to
once every two days**
YES! Unless you count V. Nasty sleepless night
experience in which I either luked in mirror
fourteen times during Adam/Candice nightmare, or
DREAMT I did. I think the thong unmanned me.

4) Limit bazoom measuring to once a week
Have got down to once daily. Still working on
vibrating machine that will get weight off nose and
vibrate it on to bazooms. Maybe cld take some of

Priscilla Crump's extra bulk if I link her up with wires to machine.

5) Only measure nose every month instead of weekly

Twice this week. Not vg. V. Unfair that childhude always spent with neat little hooter which then explodes on adolescence just when you are hoping other bitz of you will explode . . .

6) Stop reading krap magazines like *Smirk, Weenybop, Teendreems* Etck

Have luked at these now and then, ahem. Just light releef . . .

7) Read V. Good bukes to improve Mind, starting with *War and Peace*

Am on page ten.

8) Do homewerk on day it's set instead of whole week's werth on Sun at 11 pm

Ridiculous resolution. Far more imp thingz on mind.

9) Improove speling

Essentientiential.

10) Keep rume tidy

Will empty Vast Box today.

11) Be nice to Benjy
Guilt re Night-of-the-long-tubes and no burger.
Guilt assuaged through Halloween fun, sort of.

12) Save every speck of money for Granny Chubb's Spectacles Endeavour (aiming to buy her a pair for Christmas)
Had to spend money on Halloween to cheer other frendz. Must keep sense of perspectacletive.

13) Stop being superstitious
Forgot to touch wood when saw black cat on Wednesday. Good sign.

14) As above, cure one nervous habit each month, starting with having to touch the floor twice whenever I drop something
Too stressed to attend to this now. Wot does a bit of praying, touching floor Etck matter in grate scheme of things?

15) Be nice about my mother's paintings
Admired Andy Warhol style fried egg, but she said was sunset.

16) Ditto about my Adored Father's writing
Have tried to think what might be sed about the single werd 'Dolores'. Have decided, not a lot. But cld see how many werds you can make out of it: rod, door, led, red, sod, sore, role, sold, dole (this is qu

boring akshully, but I note dollars is not among them. Come to think of it, V. Worrying werds . . . don't much like wot they cld add up to).

17) Make New frendz
Cld be nice to have frend who does not cry all time . . .

18) Do not wear same pair of socks more than once
Absurd, hopeless dream. Realism new name of game.

19) Keep Up with World Events
V. Sad that ye poete laureate and author of V. Gude buke *The Iron Man* has just died. Is this world event? Also, in House of Lords only 2% are Ladies. Ban ye lotte, off with their heds sez El Chubb.

20) Add one new werd to vocabulary each day as part of on-going Self-Improvement course
Hav done loads of these.

Have woken V. Early after Bad Night with Benjy. Finally turned him over to Only Mother at 6.30 am. He always comes into my bed, never theirs. It's Not Fair.

Only Mother snored, grunted, 'Told you vampire suit wld scare him,' and went straight back to land of nod. But it wasn't Halloween that upset Benjy –

he loves that sort of thing. It's perfectly normal things like floors that upset him. And in this case, five thousand sweeties. He dreamt that floor had turned into vat of toffee . . . more difficult kind of dream for him, this one, harder to work out what he Really Feels.

Good thing about Sundays is, you know you CAN'T get a letter. E-mail must be awful, you can get it any time at all, so if you're looonging to hear from someone and don't, you don't get a moment's peace and keep turning e-mail prog on and off like light-bulb.

Weird when you think that hundreds of years ago people wld have thought it wld be bliss to be able to speak to whoever you liked whenever you wanted. *'Dear Bunty, just missed London stagecoach, so back in three weeks.' 'Dear Tesco's Provender Shoppe, please send haunch of venison and enormous turnip ASAP.'*

But the trouble with reliable and instant communications is that you haven't got the excuse of saying the postman prob got shot by highwaymen if you don't hear anything from yr Lurved One. Resign *moi*self to fact that Adam Doesn't Care and bury self in werk. Will now slope off to G. Chubb's and tidy out Vast Box on return.

G. Chubb gave me lesson on how to cook fish in various tasty ways. She was V. Shocked I shld be doing it for Rover however. Blush when I think that G. Chubb quite often buys cat food for herself to

131

eat. Arg. Wot is this werld in which posh pets eat
salmon while yumans starve? Wail, gnash, hair
shirt. Explained to G. Chubb that precious photos
will be back in her mitts next week for sure (will
bribe Harvey to copy them on Mon).

Mon Nov 2

Yet *another* PINK envelope secretly shuffled into
Adored Father's pocket this am. Needless to say, no
blue airmail one nestling amid the post . . .
   It is Bug-busting week so Nits are Public Enemy
Numero Uno – zillions of leaflets, TV progs Etck,
four letters from Benjy's skule. I'm itching already.
Don't know why they stop at potions like *Nitmare*
and *Zappalouse*. Boffins cld no doubt come up with
cruise missiles for surgical anti-nit strikes, potion-
spraying planes swooping over yr playground,
electric chairs for nits Etck. Spose the latter cld pave
the way for defence counsel for Nits Etck. Cld get
rather expensive and slow. Not sure wot Animal
Rights Position wld be on nits. Not sure wot it shld
be on Kitty, as it happens.

Spent free time in skule library poring over war bukes for inspiration for grate werk of art. Wonder if my film cld be called *War and Peace*? Or is it copyright by Leo Tolstoy & Sons Ltd PLC? *Strife and Serenity*? *Shouts & Whispers*? *Fish & Chips*? Hrrrmph. That Tolstoy knew a thing or two when it came to werds. Whole street seems to be dug up and filled with sewer blokes, cable blokes and YES! phone engineers. Still haven't found werking phone box.

Tue Nov 3
Period due.

V. Weird thing happened today. Was in library, deeply absorbed in fascinating buke of photos about Werld War Two and wondering if cld nick some of them to intercut with own grate werks, when felt strange prickling at back of neck and urge to luke out of window. My eyes, drawn as if by some strange magnetick magnetism, fell swiftly upon a group of boyz just outside. And one in particular. He was . . . about five feet 10 inches tall, eyes a mix of sea-green and ocean blue, very dark but with flecks of gold in, soft thick hair, the colour of, wait for it . . . vanilla fudge . . . Arg. Gulp. Yeeeech. Mystery Boy.

Familiar feeling of vole in headlights overwhelmed *moi*. Stood staring for wot felt like hours and then let out strange high-pitched squeak as if oncoming driver had failed to see hypnotized

133

vole and accelerated over same. I banged furiously on the window, simultaneously yelling at Aggy, who was poring over some little essay of Einstein's. 'Quick, Ags!' I screamed. 'It's him.'

Mrs Tome, the librarian, looked up in horror before surging towards us. I fled downstairs, hurtled into playground, charged round to library window. Nobody there. No Mystery boy. No boy at all. Ags, of course, had seen nothing. Where had whole group of boyz vanished to in split second? Feel V. Weird about this. Could Mystery Boy poss be an alien? Strange scar on cheek . . . spooky eyes . . . V. Odd effect on El Chubb, producing overwhelming urges on sight. Oh well, if he is an alien maybe I'll be the one he chooses to abduct. Hope so.

WELCOME!

to the Interplanetary Cosmic LURVE DOME!

LUXURIATE in our LUXURIOUS saunas
while gorgeously appealing ALIENS
do your bidding!

We specialise in OUTERCOURSE, the new OUTERSPACE LURVE TECHNIQUES that put PLEASURE FIRST! (No more unwanted babies, girls and boys!)

V. Excited re film course. Harvey has done huge enlargements of kids in rubbish pix. Must say they do luke amaaazing. Also, V. De luxe copies of Granny Chubb pix. The babe in G. Chubb's arms lukes even more adorable. Much sweeter than other pix of Dad at that age. Fantastic.

Solitary phone engineer still werking down hole. Took him sneaky cup of tea and asked with best pasted on smile if I might borrow his mobile for urgent call. He was V. Nice but stopped me after I'd dialled about eighteen digits saying the phone co might ask him why he's ringing people on the other side of the werld in werk hours and anyway his mobile doesn't ring that far. Slunk off, blushing. Well, Basil's ansaphone was on, so I thought I'd just try Mogul's L.A. Empire one more time . . .

Wed Nov 4
Birthday of Guru Nanak Dev Ji

Was barricaded in bathrume examining remarkable new spot site: little row of them neatly dotted across forehead, like lines in test where you have to fill in missing werd, when heard trilling phone closely followed by icicled chime of Only Mother announcing, 'It's a boy.' Heart pitter pattering as though a thousand mice were skeetering fairy like upon my soul.

'Letty, are you feeling better?' says V. Familiar Voice.

Blurg. The disappointment of hearing Brian's nasal tones was so crushing I cld hardly speak. Replied eventually in voice of dead trout. 'Sure.'

'Er, I just thought, as it's my birthday' (he obv said this to make me feel guilty. Why shld I remember his birthday?) 'that you might like to join me for a bite. I'm the Age of consent now and you will be too soon, har har har.'

This was so unlike Brian that I wondered if he'd been having hormone injections or investigating his dad's drinks cabinet. Stupefied with sleep and glume I couldn't think of more than ten excuses for each of the next ten daze – so agreed to go out with him on Saturday week.

Arg, why am I so soft hearted?

But then I spose Brian is to me as I am to Adam. This thort fills me with such glume that I decide to go back to bed for day, but then remember that long ago, faraway, but ever-present kiss-of-kisses that I shared with Adam (as opposed to excruciating slobber with Brian when I cut my nose on his specs) . . .

Not long passes before am called back to phone by Mother. 'A MAN, this time,' she snorts.

Yippeee! Adam or Basil both sound like MEN, not Boyz.

But it is David, Carrier of the Briefcase-of-Horror. Had I found a pair of fishnets that seem to be missing from his sizzling stash? Like shoes, hard to get in his size. Hope Only Mother isn't listening in.

Tell him I'll look.

And so to skule, gharstly period, heartbroken Aggy, sneering Syd Snoggs, Melancholy Priscilla and double detention. Must try harder with homewerk Etck. Arg.

Do science homewerk all evening instead of reading to Benjy. Tell him he'll be able to make real potions with bunsen burners when he goes to secondary skule. This make him V. Excited and am forced to read *Baby Squirrel's Birthday Treat* six times as he has regressed to bukes he enjoyed when he was two.

When Benjy finally asleep, rang Basil. Strange bloke answered and says he'll be back V. Late but will get him to ring me in morning. Go to bed in agony of anticipation.

Thurs Nov 5
Bonfire Night

Buy a few sparklers and have glumey time with Benjy in yard. Hazel rang, furious. Her dad has had three rude messages on his e-mail saying lay off my man you bitch, and he thinks it's something to do with Hazel or some weird cyberporn web site she's been visiting. (It *must* be Candice, then.)

I try to apologize, but Hazel V. Frosty. Then ice melts into routine deluge of tears. Hazel's folks are having their usual huge firework party on Sat. Mandy not sure she can come down from Scotland. All is glume and dume. My turn to feel frosty. Have had only lonely sparklers with Benjy and now my Best Frend is not asking me to her bonfire party. Oh well, just one more person who Doesn't Care . . . pretend something burning on stove to get off phone before sobs of self pity threaten to engulf *moi*. This crying thing obv V. Contagious. Wonder if there is a pill blokes take. You never see them in tears on phone to frendz.

Two mins later, Hazel rings back to check that I'm going to her firework party. Well of course she asked me before, how could I have forgotten? Realize this is white lie, but also realize she does V. Much want me to go, if only to hold Mandy-less mitt.

Line of little spotz on forehead has extended. First ones have turned greenish, ones at end of row are puce. Odd symmetry about them. Praps rays from laser of Mystery Boy, attempting to beam me up to sexshual experimentation centre . . .

Fri Nov 6
Film Course, 7.30

Whole day in agony of anticipation, glume Etck because e-mail scuppered and No Other News. At lunchtime, decided to reveal all to Aggy.

'Well, the obvious thing to do is . . .' she started, when Priscilla sat down next to us, sobbing.

'I can't go on like this.' Sniff sniff bawl.

'Oh, poooor Cilla,' said Aggy, overflowing with the milk of human kindness. I just felt V. Pissed off and stomped off. How dare Priscilla Crump just plonk herself down? Spose she does have a Bun in the Oven, so what? Couldn't she see we had something important to talk about?

Was slightly cheered by Film Skule. I secretly believe that Alfonsa Rosselini reckons my project is the best. Dot says it is far and awaaay the best.

'You know, Letty, you've reeally got your Hed screwed on? This is just the best?' (I put in the question marks because, like all Australians, she makes statements that go up at the end like questions.) But it is V. Nice to be bathed in flattery; my other frendz are just so obsessed with their own probs at the moment, or Priscilla Crump's . . . She tells me I shld visit Australia, sez there can be V. Interesting opportunities in The Artz there. I say, to luke Kule, I'm thinking of going to L.A. first.

'Why? You got a little twinkle out there? I said, you got a little twinkle out there?'

Realize it is a question this time and mumble 'Yes', adding in V. Fakely modest tones, 'Hollywood actually. My boyfriend works for Mogul Mogul Junior the Third.'

'No? Not Mogul!? Mogul Mogul Junior the

Third? Hollywood Leg End? Maker of *Mission Interminable, Relatives of the Lost Clerk, Reservoir Bloggs, Erratic Quark* and the soon to be released *Anville?*'

'Um, yes. That Mogul.'

Soon this news was all round the room and people were looking at me with new respeck. I think.

Arg. Just as I was writing the above, at 11 pm, Basil rang. Adam is coming home *Saturday.*

'So, party starts around 9.00. Gottit? Tell the others.'

'Er, sure. Are you sure?'

'Sure what?'

'Sure he's coming back? Tomorrow?'

'Sure I'm sure. See ya.'

I can't believe it. Adam! Tomorrow! But do I dare go? He hasn't written . . . but that's obv cos Candice is sabotaging my letters, same way as she sabotaged my e-mail. Of course I will go. Will create amazing impact in leopardskin leotard. Or leotard-skinned leopard. Or something. Will go, of course.

But have just remembered Awful Thing. I promised to go to Hazel's fireworks party. How is it that you can go for years Shunned By the Social Werld, Spat on by destiny Etck and then have zillions of commitments for the same day? How can I desert my best frend who is heartbroken over her only absent gurlfrend to go to Basil's (who I don't even KNOW) in the hopes of re-uniting with

Adam, who will prob be locked in the arms of Nono Nymphette anyway?

BUT, I convince myself with lightning speed of lightning, maybe cld make BOTH parties? Basil sed, come after NINE. But Hazel's doesn't start till late either. Arg. Worry, Worry. Will think about it tomorrow.

Sat Nov 7

Eventually realized the inevitable. Rang Hazel, sick with nerves, glad it was only her mum and not her I had to tell I was feeling awful (true) and didn't think I'd be able to make it (also true).

Felt frolicsome with relief after this fibette. It's like when you get yr Poor Harassed Caring Adult to say you're out to someone you don't want to meet when you're just cowering outside the back door. It's a lie, but it's kind of true, too.

But with Hazel getting her own party ready and Aggy going to Hazel's there is no-one I can ask advice about wot to wear. Decide to pluck up courage to ask Only Mother. Seeing I am a bag of nerves, she cheerfully replies, 'It's only Hazel's.' More Guilt.

'Yeh, but you know . . .'

'But it's fireworks, Letty,' sed my mum. 'Your lovely new coat and a pair of wellies would be fine . . .'

That shld set his pulses racing: nylonette coat-of-glume and welly boots. Still, there's no accounting for the tastes of Boyz, and anyway underneath am wearing V. Daring black lacy number that used to be a slip. Never worn anything like it before but never wanted moment like this so much either. Nick some of my Only Mother's tights before realizing I have no proper shoes that go with a dress. Reckon black plimsolls will

How to set his pulses racing

have to do and wld akshully luke quite kule, like I haven't been trying too hard. Stuff them in voluminous pocket of nylonette coat-of-glume. At least it's good for something.

I tried various things with my wig to no avail. I can sometimes make it luke qu nice for about five seconds, but sadly it always has the same face hanging underneath it.

Finally slunk out of house, feeling dodgy as had not eaten thing all day except mouthful of Galactic Snaks from Benjy's breakfast bowl.

It was freezing cold and I breathed steamy sigh of thanks into icy fog for amazing warmth of coat-of-glume. Basil's is only a short bus ride away but I was so scared that someone might recognize me at bus stop and wonder why I'm not at Hazel's that I went round a V. Long way, walking. Spose this V. Typical Teenage Worrier's behaviour, daft except for the terrific sense it makes when you're akshully doing it.

Got V. Twitchy at sound of any footsteps behind me in gharstly freezing underlit Urban wastescape as approached dreade Gradgrind Estate. Benjy's frend Bugsy and his little brother Duane live here, and there are always stories about people being mugged, murdered, boiled alive and eaten.

Then . . . as I am walking down narrow passage, hear horrific scream and the sound of breaking glass. Freeze in terror. Silence, then more screaming. Wot to do? Run for it? Run for help? Run towards the sound, risk banana in heroick rescue attempt? Every second seemed like a year, a year whose seconds were long, to paraphrase ye grate Oscar Wilde . . .

Suddenly there was a clatter of footsteps and a young woman clasping a wailing child came hurtling towards me.

'What's wrong?' I stuttered, peering into shadows for emerging yeti-like figure with axe.

'Leave it out, you interfering cow,' says hurtling figure, slowing a little. 'Darren's cut hisself nicking a radio. Chemist shuts at ten.'

I am never going to walk through the Gradgrind Estate on my own after dark, ever again, even if there aren't any yetis with axes.

Emerge into brightly lit throng of pubs, late-nite shops Etck, feeling V. Groggy. Leant on lamppost to recover and was approached by V. Posh-luking man in raincoat. 'How much?' he arsked, in a voice like Prince Charles.

Distinct feeling that this Was Not My Night. Turned and fled towards Basil's street. Had timed it well. 9.35. Took deep breath, rearranged wig in wing mirror of parked car, saw person's hand inside emerging from shadowy places in clothing of companion not normally seen by El Chubb except in videos 'borrowed' by Hazel from parents' box misleadingly labelled 'French New Wave', and finger thereon being lifted in unmistakable message.

Hastily moved away, slipped off nylonette coat-of-glume (hoping against hope that Prince Charles sound-alike was not luming round corner), stuffed willies, sorry wellies, in capacious pocket of same, stuffed feet into plimsolls and strolled casually towards number 38.

House completely dark. Maybe it was a surprise party and everyone was in there waiting to snap on lights and shout 'Welcome Adam! We lurve you!' Cheered by this thought I rang bell.

No reply.

Basil must have said ten o clock then. He must have, I thought, biting lip and holding back tear. Or had I got the house number wrong? Or the street? But no. I checked my little bit of paper three times. Shld I wait until ten and try again? Shld I go to Hazel's? But it wld take me half an hour to get to Hazel's even if a bus came quickly. Arg. Wot a hopeless fule was I. Decided the best thing was to wait. But where? Scared of being approached by more government Ministers slumming it Etck, I decided to sit on Basil's steps. Not for the first time on this gharstly nite-of-icy-drizzle, I was V. Releeeved to be accompanied by the solar pannelled coat-of-glume which was almost beginning to feel like a faithful frend.

Dear reader, I'm sure you can guess that as the hours ticked **dolorously** by (NB **New Werd**: meaning sadly, but unfortunately putting me in mind of the mystery Dolores), my mind was filled with nagging doubt. Even if a party starts V.V. Late, the hosts are usually inside getting ready by this time, putting Twiglets in saucers Etck.

At 10.42 I mournfully picked frozen self up and trailed homeward, taking even longer route to avoid Gradgrind. Walked in middle of road most of time, to dodge kerb crawlers and being solicited. Amazing wot you can luke like and still get picked up, isn't it? Makes you wonder why gurlz go to so much trouble, shaving leg and underarm wigs, deforesting eyebrows, reforesting eyelashes, anointing selves with unguents, war paint Etck. Finally arrive home, frozen to marrow, shaking like aspen and starving like parched mariner on frozen ocean at 11.15 pm.

'Nice party?' sez Only Mother through clenched teeth.

'Great,' I lie through clencheder teeth.

'Basil rang to say his party was off as Adam's flight was delayed. But I told him you'd gone to another party.'

Silence. Long, heavy laden silence. Clock ticked somewhere. Mother spoke again. 'Who's Basil?'

'Oh, some bloke.'

'Who's Adam?'

'Oh, some other bloke.'

Leaden silence, more weighty than the first. 'Scarlett. Did you go to Hazel's?'

'Not exactly.'

I stormed off to rume before any more questions could pour from twisted lip of irate parent. To my grate surprise could hear gentle tones of Adored Father, poss lubricated by calming influence of Old Bastard Lager. 'She'll calm down. Love troubles. Teenage Years. Periods. Etck.'

Will now attempt to fall into glumey, starved, tossing sleep. Realize Syd Snoggs wld have something he reckons Dead Funny to say about this statement, but too tired to rewrite it . . .

Sun Nov 8
Remembrance Sunday

Adam now coming on Wed, it turns out. Basil says he's now having a little 'drinks do' for then and that Adam said it would be nice to see me.

'Y-you m-m-mentioned me?'

'Sure. Why not? Adam likes to see old pals.'

'Er, he didn't give you any other message?'

'Nope.'

'Mmmmblgt.'

'Huh?'

'Myaahsplurfnnnnaaaahhahaha.'

'Sure. Bye.'

Basil obv thinks I am original lune from mune.

Hazel rang a few minutes later, as I was half way into my second packet of Galactic Snaks, and all the way into trance of anticipation. Galactic Snaks are the only things in the house that my mother buys in bulk, cos they are Benjy's favourite. She never does the same with fudge . . .

Hazel V. Upset that I wasn't at her party and Mandy wasn't either. Does anyone care, she thinks? Small peeper-opener to El Chubb that someone of Hazel's qualities can feel like this too. Wanted to tell her whole truth, but instead told her about Wed and my hopes of true lurve rekindling. She showed V. Little understanding.

Too knackered to go round to G. Chubb's.

Have just remembered it is Remembrance Sunday and didn't even be quiet for the Minute's silence. Wot kind of War Film will I ever make? Gnash.

147

Mon Nov 9

Spend day on wings of hope, Even double detention and fart spray in the loos (Sandra Snoggs, Syd's orrible sister again) cannot dampen my youthful spirits buoyed up on wings of hope . . . Only blow was, I noticed another PINK envelope. Grabbed it off mat, but before I had the chance to check for perfume, curly handwriting, S.W.A.L.K.s scrawled on back Etck, it was whisked from my mitt by irate Father.

'MINE I think,' he snarled.

It is the first time I have seen him snarl and blush at once. Arg.

Tue Nov 10

Can think of nothing but seeing Adam on Wed.

Aggs says, 'Basil's OK. Known him since I was three. Shall I come with you?'

YES. Brill if Aggy comes. Also, she sez a party will cheer HER up, as she is feeling lousy about her mum.

Wed Nov 11

Veteran's Day USA. Remembrance day, Canada
Babysit

6 am. Woken up in cold sweat. *Aaargh, yeechgg, blaarrrk.* Today is Babysitting Nite.

Shook Only Mother awake and BEGGED her to let me go out, just for an hour. No joy. Instead she launches into her usual let's-start-from-here-and-talk-about-everything whinge. Shld have let her know before. Why can't I be more organized? Why do I think the werld revolves around me? My room's a mess. I'll get no GCSEs and have to spend life cleaning toilets. Where did we go wrong? Anyway this evening cld be big break for Dad blah blah.

'Why can't Dad go on his own then? I'll only be out till about 9.30. Please please please,' I begged and pleaded with them both but couldn't bring myself to explain exactly why I needed to go out so badly. Said it was cos I didn't want to let down a frend. Felt hot shame at this but anyway it was no good. Mother said they have to be at Vital Publisher's fancy thingy at 7.30 on dot, and it's time I grew up and took responsibility and thought about other people for a change. Blah blah blah, continued from Episode One. Doesn't she care AT ALL about her only female offspring?

Went like slug to skule, but pondering devious plotte to get Aggy to babysit since she doesn't *need* to go to party anyway. Good old Aggy, she doesn't mind at all about missing the party to babysit. She is the gratest.

Shld be time between parents going out and Aggy arriving for fabulous bubble bath Etck before slipping into slinky slip and slipping out into inky night-of-promise . . .

Wot a night.

Begins with El Chubb struggling to shove parents out of house before innocent Aggy arrives to babysit. Impossible, of course — usual stuff people do when you desperately want them to be somewhere else: come back for missing handbags, keys, credit cards, last visit to loo, make sure eye make-up isn't running down nose Etck.

Aggy arrived at 7.40, ever the Good Frend.

'Oh, Aggy. Poor love,' says Only Mother anxiously. 'Didn't Letty tell you she wasn't going to the party? We'll take you.'

'But I've come to babysit,' said Aggy, innocently.

All hell breaks loose, of course.

'Not want pooooey Aggy!' wailed Benjy, tactfully, from behind the sofa.

'Benjy, how could you? Aggy's like a sister to you!' I yelled.

Aggy stood, bemused, shuffling on the doorstep.

'Come on, Aggy, we'll take you to the party. Disgraceful behaviour,' my mother sniffed. My father threw me an anxious luke and they swept out, sweeping poor Aggy with them.

Hurled self onto sofa, sobbing.

'Letto, wot wrong? Not like staying in with Benjy?' wailed Benjy, pitifully, in my uncaring ear . . .

Seconds later there was a ferocious banging on the door. I leant out the window and shouted, 'Stop all that row, you'll wake the Rottweiler.' But the banging continued.

''Sonly us' said a pathetic sounding voice, so I opened the door a crack to see Kev and Nev, the two nerdish thirteen-year-old boyz from down the road. 'Our gerbil's got out. He's in your front garden.'

'Kev, Nev, hi. Wait a minute.'

Kev took a drag on his fag and immediately went into paroxysms of coughing and dropped it. He and Nev then dived full length onto the doormat at my feet.

'He's gone inside well fast. Fag must've dropped on him. He's pissed off already cos I gotta fruit-bat now.'

'Who is?' I asked.

'The gerbil,' said Nev contemptuously. 'We gotta come in and get him.'

A light-bulb of hope glowed above the slowly turning wheels of my brain. 'Of course you have, of course you have. My brother'll help you look.'

'What, that little one?'

'Yes, Benjy.'

Kev looked doubtful: 'Gerbil's big as him.'

'All the better!' I yelled triumphantly. 'Put him at his ease! Look . . .' I now put on my most confidential and conspiratorial voice, 'can you keep a secret?'

'No,' they chorused, like Tweedledum and Tweedledee.

But I wasn't going to be stopped now. I hurtled, unthinking, on: 'Well never mind, I want the world to know my pain. My parents have locked me in here because I wanted to go and meet a . . . a boy . . . you know. My father's consumed with jealousy. If you stayed here with Benjy for an hour, I could go and meet him. It's . . . it's for love. You know . . .'

'Urgh. Yeeeccch.'

'Well, it's passion. Like *Titanic*.'

'Can we watch?'

'No!' I said, outraged despite *moi*self, and therefore losing a crucial advantage. The nerds shrugged, lost interest and went on looking for the gerbil. I'm afraid to say I compromised. 'But I could tell you about it.'

'All right,' said Kev. 'Just a coupl'ov hours though.'

'That's all we need.' I winked suggestively.

'Don't go down the takeaway after, do you?' shouted Nev.

'No, sorry.' On second thoughts I hunted round and gave them two mangey biscuits and, with grate difficulty, a bag of fudge.

'There's stuff in the fridge,' I added, hopefully. 'Help yourselves.' Then, before I could think second thoughts, I wheeled out my trusty bike. I wasn't risking being picked up as hooker Etck again.

'Letto? Where you going?' were the pathetic werds I heard Benjy squeak as I ruthlessly and without ruth raced out the front door. 'Want to come wiv you, Letto. Not leave me here with pooey Nev'n'Kev! Where you going? Letto, wait!'

Telling myself I wld be half an hour at most, I pedalled furiously into night.

Basil's house was ablaze with light . . .

A vast bloke with dreadlocks who was also about eight feet tall and eight feet wide opened the door. So this was Basil. Sounds of carousing, heavy metal Etck so loud I could hardly hear *moi*self speak.

'Letty,' I yelled.

'Oh yeh. Come in. Have a drink.'

Flat was heaving with sweaty bodies. Fought my way through to kitchen, looking desperately for a hint of blackberry curls. Nothing. Downed two cokes in five seconds and felt slightly strange. God! What was in them? Eville drugges?

Felt trapped in sea of surging bods for wot seemed like hours, feeling distinctly queasy. The vast form of Basil hove into view. Tottered after him into strange swaying rume. Noticed the ceiling was carpeted in odd orange swirls.

'Sh'veryodd. Whass a carpet doin onner floor?' I

thought. Not sure how much later it was that I pushed something big and furry off me (a bearskin rug? A pet?). Someone was offering me a glass of something.

'No. Sheville druggsh.'

'Come on, it's water,' said Basil.

The limpid liquid coursed through my veins, I think. I splashed it on my face. Phew.

'Where's Adam?'

'Oh. Fraid he's left. Had to babysit his little sister. You all right?'

'He'd rather be with his baby sister?'

'Rather than what?' said Basil, quizzically. 'He's crazy about her.'

I turned and fled. It is hard to describe, dear reader, the depths to which my soul plummeted as I pedalled home, weaving maniacally through the dume-laden urban wastescape. Two fantasies surged through my fevered brain.

The first was one in which a TV presenter was making an announcement: '*And this year's Mr Nice Guy Award for Brains, Beauty and Heart goes to . . . Adam Stone.*' (Applause. Followed by pix of Adam reading nursery rhymes to his adorable sister. Fire glowing in grate.)

This gave over to terrifying Fantasy Two: Benjy was crying 'Lettoooo, Lettoooo' amid clouds of smoke. There was a tabloid headline: TOT FACES INFERNO ALONE! I wished I was dead.

I pedalled furiously, vast coat-of-glume flapping, cars skidding around me. Had I known what Worry was till now? I had to abandon the bike. I wrecked it. I've never run so far or so fast in my life. As I turned into our street I heard sirens and knew the house would be ablaze.

And it was.

Every light in every window was on. Kev and Nev had taken the search for the gerbil very seriously.

I went in to find Nev, Kev and Benjy in a row on the sofa, watching the telly.

'Lo! Lettish!' Benjy drawled, his face a nasty shiny red like a battered tomato.

'Benjy, I love you.' I clutched him to me, slowly taking in the scene around me. Kev, Nev and Benjy were each clutching a can of lager. They were watching *Terminator II*.

The flood of relief was followed by a wave of horror. Alive! But drunk.

'Benjy. What have they *done* to you?' I swept him into my arms. 'How dare you let him watch this krap? He's FIVE!'

'It's a PG,' said Nev.

'Liar.'

'You asked us to look after him.'

'You're drinking beer! How can you be so irresponsible?'

'You told us to help ourselves,' said Kev. 'Anyway, it was for medicinal reasons, innit? He's gone mental about something he saw on the carpet, but he was all right after we give him a drink like.'

I spent the next half hour crazily tidying up the repellent remains of Kev and Nev's visit. Crisps, gerbil poo and melting ice-cream covered every surface. Was just hustling poor old Benjy upstairs when dreaded parents arrived.

'Hellooo Mummy and Daddy,' Benjy crowed triumphantly from the landing. 'Not scared of floors any more. Kev an' Nev give me nice medicine.'

I clapped my hand over the long suffering Benjy's mush and hurtled on. 'Yes, Kev from down the road and his mate came round looking for their gerbil, and they were so nice to Benjy, I was really surprised . . .'

Mother shot Father a withering look. There was a resounding belch from Benjy.

I soldiered on . . . 'And Benjy ate too much fudge so he's feeling a bit funny in his tummy, aren't you Benjy?'

Benjy brought a lager can I hadn't spotted from underneath his Winnie The Pooh pyjama top and waved it in Father's direction. 'Cheers,' was all he said.

I have been grounded for a week. Which means no film course.

Nothing else matters. Surprising how much Benjy liked beer. I've never been able to understand why adults drink it.

Note it is Remembrance Day all over the werld. Try to think of Veterans Etck, but can only think of fulish self and mourn my One true lurve.

Thurs Nov 12

At lunch break I poured what was left of my heart (now a pale biscuity thing, where once it had been plump, bouncy, vermilion, pumping with vigour) out to Aggs.

'And to think, he left early to look after his baby sister,' I was just saying when a nasty clanging voice interrupted.

'Candice looks young all right,' said the voice, 'but you'd have to be a mug to take her for his baby sister. Not if this is him.' We had been overheard by horrible Syd's horrible sibling, Sandra Snoggs, who was waving a copy of *Long Lens*, the krap film gossip mag.

Oh God. Syd and Sandra have an even more horrible third sibling, Dion 'Grotto' Snoggs, who's a nightclub bouncer. They say he has to stay on the door cos he's too big to get in. Last night Dion told Sandra that Adam was at the Liquid Cortex club dancing the night away . . .

With Candice Carthage.

Anyway, I was about to hit Sandra but sensible Aggy got her to reveal (not that she needed much

158

persuading) what she'd read in *Long Lens* about
blockbuster producer Mogul Mogul Jnr III, over
here for a couple of days with his family including
stunning (yeeech) daughter Candice to collect some
Lifetime Achievement Award from Brit film
organization on telly. It's all terrible. So that's why
Adam is here. With her!

But wait. A glimmer of hope still flickered. 'I bet
it WASN'T Adam at the Liquid Cortex,' I said.
'How would old Dion know who Adam was?'

'Well he told me he'd seen Candice. *Everyone*
knows HER,' crowed Sandra. 'And said she was
snogging someone, and I said, "Was it this bloke?"'
And then Sandra waved *Long Lens* under my nose
and I nearly fainted. There, *holding hands* with the
dread Candice, was blackberry curled, lissom limbed
. . . Adam, looking more dazzling, winsome,
glimmering Etck than ever.

So he obviously left Basil's early because he didn't
want Candice to get all snotty about meeting his
grubby frendz from his former life like *moi*, and told
Basil he was babysitting so as not to offend
everybody. But really he was only interested in
clutching Candice at every opportunity, even over
here, when he could be rediscovering Who He
Really Is and getting away from the tawdry values of
tinseltown. Dust, ashes, overwhelming glume.

I write this with Rover on my lap. Her power to
comfort me fades as my hormones mone.

Fri Nov 13
(ARG Superstition Etck)
Film Course 7.30

Friday 13th. Despair. Glume. Raging fever.
Attempt to rise from bed of pain causes strange
jangling in head. Brain has clearly been replaced by
small troupe of chickens playing xylophones. Missed
skule. Banned from film course by raging parents
but wld have missed it anyway . . .

Sat Nov 14

Raging fever. At 7.30 doorbell rang. Mother opened
it to reveal freshly pressed Brian with vast bunch of
chrysanthemums, which I hate, some of which were
also freshly pressed by Only Mother, who closed the
door on Brian before he was completely in.

I had forgotten all about date with Brian. Told
Only Mother not to bring him into sordid bedrume
on any account, which shows what Pride can do,
because it might have been the best move I could
have made to stop him ever coming near *moi* again.
Tottered to Hed of stairs engulfed in duvet and told
him I was dying. He sed he'd call round to see how I
was if still alive on Tue. I said it wld def be too late
by then, but if the rest of the flowers were still alive
he cld scatter them on my grave. Had just enuf
energy to phone Basil again in vain faint hope that

Sandra Snoggs might, just might, be wrong. Basil out. Left pathetick message.

Sun Nov 15

Fever of body **abating** (NB **New Werd**: meaning lessening), but fever of soul raging. Phoned Basil V. Early. He confirmed my werst fears re Candice. Didn't I know? he asked. Silence. Then Basil suddenly sounded V. Tender.

'You've, er, got a bit of a thing about him, haven't you?'

Silence. Sobs. Muffled, hiccupping gulps and gurgles.

Basil told me that Adam was only here for few days. Taking his mum (aah . . . me . . . he's kind to his mum) and Candice to Mogul Mogul's awards thingy . . . (So Sandra Snoggs had it absolutely right, the biche.) He said he thought it better I shld forget about Adam. He's sure I'm a grate person and will find lurve elsewhere, Etck.

Was heartbroken, but touched. Can't help thinking that if Basil wasn't Olde Man of about thirty, he wld be V. Nice person to fall in lurve with. So understanding. Even if he is eight foot tall and ten foot wide.

Mon Nov 16

Still ill. Pretend to be iller still. Can't face skule,
Sandra Snoggs, Priscilla Crump Etck. ANOTHER
pink envelope for Dad. V. Worried.

Worried also about spotz. Worried about nose.
Worried about having no bazooms. Worried about
state of Soul. Worried about parents' relationship.
Worried about homewerk. Worried about whether
my fever is terminal illness just disguised as flu.
Worried about giant asteroid plummeting toward
Earth. Worried about inability of yumankind to live
in peace. Worried that, with my life at lowest ebb,
Rover will die and leave me frendless without frend
in werld.

Tue Nov 17

Slobbed around in dressing-gown wailing,
Worrying and getting under Mother's feet. She sez I
must go to skule tomorrow and illness
psychoticomatic, or something (**New Werd**: must
look it up, prob means one day I will attack
somebody in shower with rolled-up copy of *Smirk*).

After glumey supper of pot noodle had just curled
up with Rover in front of telly when faithful Brian
called round with wilting bunch of daisies. Mad
Mother let him in 'to cheer me up'. He plonked self
down next to *moi* on sofa, just as the *Barry Normal*

Film Show came on, announcing they were going straight to the Shitz Hotel for live luvvie coverage including Lifetime Achievement Award for Mogul Mogul Junior the Third.

My heart started wild cluster of throbbing and my eyes were on stalks, causing Brian to get wrong impression, so was forced to push large cushion between us. Curled up in foetal position, squinting at screen through fingers, dreading the werst.

And there was Mogul Mogul Junior the Third. Getting medal put round his oak-like neck by young mermaid in silver sheath. Mogul Mogul Junior Third is a vast block of a man with voice like diesel engine, oozing dynamism, cynicism, egotism, hedonism, dogmatism, cannibalism and every other self-indulgent or downright dangerous kind of ism you can think of, and leering lasciviously at anything that moves and is under 25 (apparently this includes dogs and cats as well as boyz and gurlz, but my publisher may censor this as libellous).

He droned on and on about how he was born in matchbox at bottom of sewer Etck and struggled to feed his ten starving siblings with his earnings as a shoeshine boy in the Bronx. As he was gazing at his poor pinched face in the patent leather shoe of a surly millionaire, he had a Vision of a Better Life, which led to his first major werk: *Armageddon Outa here*.

Since when, he has climbed from strength to strength and made more MONEY (he lingers long on the werd, rolling his eyes like Long John Silver) than the patent leather millionaire will ever see! The camera at this point panned round the glowing tear-stained faces of the cheering, weeping celebrity audience. El Chubb, meanwhile, fought against urge to throw up, having heard quite different though equally heartrending story of Mogul's origins and realizing he made it all up – but then the camera stopped, at Candice!

Mogul was saying: 'And now I would like my lovely daughter, who will inherit the Mogul Empire, to join me onstage.' Arg. Candice was flickering along the aisle, a vision of twinkling navel and dazzling pout . . . and on her arm was . . . Adam. Mogul's drone reached a crescendo, and since that seems impossible you can get some idea what a penetrating drone it was – and then yet another dame dressed in flimsy spangles draped a medallion over his vast nut.

But I was now weeping uncontrollably and copiously into Brian's hanky.

There was Adam. MY Adam. As byootiful as the dawn in his fresh, open-necked, cream pleated shirt. His hair a mass of blackberry curls. His eyes agleam, his teeth dazzling in the footlights, the footlights dazzling on his teeth . . .

I was vaguely aware of Brian muttering something about how wonderfully sensitive I was, to be so moved by the tale of Mogul's deprived childhood.

Then, through my haze of tears, I heard Adam's voice.

What was he saying? WHAT?

I couldn't believe my ears.

Adam grabbed the microphone and shouted something that sounded like, 'This system stinks' before being hustled off by two colossal bouncers. Seconds later, we were backstage with a yoof TV presenter excitedly telling us that upstart wannabe Adam Stone, Candice's latest squeeze, had wrecked the ceremony and they were hoping to get an interview.

I could scarcely credit what had happened. Had my fevered imagination invented it? But no, there was a tear-stained Candice. There was a furious Mogul, his face contorted with frenzy. There was Barry Normal 'returning to the studio' to discuss the 'extraordinary events' at the awards ceremony with a 'panel of experts' including Black Rapping film maker Sassy G. Smythe-Smith, Feminist guru Angelica Fluff and Hed of the Keep Films Clean campaign, Winston Dread.

Suddenly became aware of cold, clammy animal crawling about under my dressing-gown. Yeecch! Screamed at Benjy that I would kill him if he had brought slugs in from the yard again to torture dying sister in her last hours, then realized it was Brian's hand which had been taking advantage of total absorption of *moi* in events on telly. He seemed almost as surprised to find it there as *moi* but threw him out anyway, telling him doctor suspected I had caught a disease that gives teenage boyz green willies.

Panel of experts all talked about themselves, or the movies they were plugging if they were involved in any, and not the events of the night at all. But then they whisked back to exclusive yoof presenter and a V. Tousled Adam, claiming that Hollywood was a sham and everyone worshipped Money and he was one day going to make films for truth justice Etck, before being pulled out of view again by vast bouncers. Arg. Will they beat him up? He's only eighteen . . .

Will Candice prove herself werthy of Adam by standing by him and renouncing her father? I hope not, oh, oh, oh how I hope it. And so, seething with a thousand questions, my hopes burning anew, to bed.

NB Threw pride to winds after trying to luke up psychoticomatic in dictionary. Only Mother pointed out it's **psychosomatic**, meaning 'all in the mind'. Is that what Worry is also?

Wed Nov 18
Babysit

Dragged self to skule in turmoil of emotions. Priscilla not there. No-one knows where she is. Feel faint throb of Worry that she has hurled herself off bridge. Aggy V. Amazed by story about Film

Awards. Sez it *could* be V. Good news, and almost makes up for not getting the babysitting money. Feel V. Bad about that, cos of course I had to thrust my pittance into the open maws of Nev and Kev who had started demanding overtime by the time I got back. Will make it up to her somehow.

Amazing news following usual hopeful call to Basil on my return home.

Adam coming home for good! Candice broken off with him! (Not surprising really, lucky Mogul Mogul hasn't broken bitz off Adam that wld make going out with anybody unnecessary ever again. He has certainly not been thinking about safeguarding His Future, but that is the kind of amazingly Passionate and Impulsive Person he is, sigh, mone.)

Basil sez he mentioned me to Adam. Aaaargh, pain, glume, raised hopes . . . He even apparently dropped a Hint that I cared. How cld he? Why did he? Thank God. He said there was a long silence and then Adam had said I had gone off with someone else and that he hadn't heard from me (WOT happened to that last letter?). But he was V. Quiet again for a moment and then said, 'Tell her I'll write.' Oh, Joy.

He goes back to the States to sort thingz out, including convincing authorities that he has not wasted his young director course bursary, and comes back in three weeks. Agony of anticipation.

Benjy had nightmare in which a vast alcoholic gerbil burst out of the floor, breath aflame, telling

167

him that he was neglecting Horace. He then got up at 10.30 to talk to Horace, who simply went round on his wheel looking as per usual.

'We should get Horace a frend. He's lonely,' said Benjy.

'I'll get you another for Christmas,' I said, in a rash rush of sisterly lurve. Two gerbils can hardly be more boring than one.

Finally got Benjy back to bed and then werked into nite on film script. Bed at three am, having made, I think, deep and serious and meaningful statement about War, Peace, Age, Youth, Despair Etck. Realize I am writing this grate werk for Adam . . .

Thurs Nov 19

Shld be knackered after nearly sleepless night, but up like lark. Only shows how much the state of yr BOD has to do with state of yr SOUL.

Spent whole day in blissful mude: totally cheerful, bright as button, fresh as new-mown hay. Can't wait to get back to film course, will toil like dervish to impress Adam – er, I mean, to learn to express *moi*self freely, emerge as Letitia Chubbantino, change art of film-making for ever, inspire yuman race with such Moving Images that all peoples of werld live happily ever after Etck. And then impress Adam, ahem.

THE ACE

Ace!

BASEMENT JAXX

LETITIANA
CHUBBIANTO
STORMS
OSCARS

inside
EXCLUSIVE
interview
with new
comet of
BRIT-FILM

PLUS:
How to
cook with
Granny
Chubb

OPEN ALL HOURS! LARRY FLYNT'S PORN SUPERMARKET CHAIN

Fri Nov 20
Film Course, 7.30

Grate film course. Alfonsa Rosselini likes my stuff.
Sez I am nearly there.

People who are meant to be inspiring you to New
Heightz say this a lot, I find. What is Nearly There?
They usually mean you would be There already if
only you hadn't started from Here, moan, whinge,
mop brow . . .

Anyway, she suggests various rewrites, and her understanding of what I am on about leads me to feel more positive about her ideas. I have growing feeling she likes my film best and begin to feel V. Happy. The other studentz films are:

1) a V. Soppy (I think) romance betwixt a streetperson living in Tesco's bag Etck and a rich gurl (sort of like *Pretty Woman* but the other way round)

b) a V. Gude one about eville drugges, in which a gurl slides down slippery slope from one fag to heroin addiction and dies a horrible banana (V. Gritty)

*) a V. Ambitious comedy about a Prince who disguises himself as a homeless person and declares the end of the monarchy as a result of his harrowing experiences among his poorer subjects (they have made the actor up to luke exactly like Prince Charles with big fake ears). V. Funny. But posh Gareth Spool, whose project this is, keeps trying to get larfs by arsking Prince to take his kit off in fit of angwish at state of poor. Kind of *Full Monty* meets *King Lear*

3, or is it 4?) a V. Sweet story about a gurl who wins London marathon (WITHOUT a wheelchair) despite being born with only one leg

e) a V. Dull but V. Werthy story about the collapse of the button-making industry called Sew Wot?

You can tell Alfonsa Rosselini has a V. Developed Social Conscience. She has picked all the films with

Deep Meaning and none of the slash 'em, burn 'em and shoot 'em up variety that a lot of the blokes wanted to make. However, it is tempting to feel that they wld have been more fun to look at if the blokes had just been left to get on with it.

It is V. Difficult telling these sort of stories in three minutes and I feel we are all lerning a Lot from each other Etck and it's just how lerning ought to be but hardly ever is. MY film is the only real true-life documentary. Also, only one shot entirely in stills, due to Chubb family poverty, ergo absence of flash video kit, but it puts unusual emphasis on soundtrack, and Alfonsa sez closing pix of the tiny kids in rubbish are fantastic climax. Espesh as they are true-life, real, contemporary tiny kidz! Asleep in the street! Covered in newspapers! Did we fight two werld wars for this? Etck. This is REAL documentary, using gritty cutting edge images from LIFE. I like to think it will say more than the dramas . . .

We're filming two of the other films next week. I have small part in eville drugges one and even smaller part in Royal Family one. The week after, we record soundtracks (I get priority). Friday eleventh we put everything together ready for BIG DAY, final showing of films to hed of film skule, mums dads Etck.

And . . . Adam WILL be there (Hope . . . hope . . .).

Sat Nov 21

Spent most of day re-writing film, choosing musick Etck. How grate is Art . . .

Sun Nov 22

Made flapjacks with G. Chubb. Took home whole pile which Benjy and me ate in front of telly with enuf maple syrup to dissolve every tooth in our heads. Thought that one day I wld be cuking these for my large family (two boyz the image of Adam and two gurlz the image of Adam) in our log cabin overluking mountain and decorated with the *Alternative Oscars* we have won for our V. Deep and Meaningful films about Truth, Byooty and Justice Etck. Hope Rover will live to see the day . . .

Mon Nov 23

Another pink envelope for Dad. He looks V. Furtive when he picks these up and, however hard I try (my mind, of course, on lower, I mean higher thingz) he always beats me to the doormat. Do I have the courage to ask him about it? Thing is, he and Only Mother seem to be rubbing along quite well and have only had two major rows this week. Maybe shld let sleeping dogs lie.

Priscilla Crump gave birth to twins in the bath this morning is the latest skule news. She's called them, obv in state of post-natal **euphoria** (NB **new werd**, meaning kind of mad bliss), Rabina and Barin. Hope she will think better of this so they can hold their little heds up without thinking of soft drinks and medicines every time someone calls their names.

Hope she will also be happy now she has two little crumpets, but I wouldn't fancy the responsibility *moi*self. Cleaning out Horace's cage and opening a can for Rover is about as much as I can manage. Whole class made Priscilla a vast card and felt V. Guilty we hadn't paid her more attention, though maybe somebody somewhere is also feeling guilty they paid Priscilla as much attention as they obviously did. Wonder who?

Other amazing news is, Daniel Hope is free again. Has junked his gurlfrend, Ozzie temptress Spiggy. Spiggy arrived this morning with vast black circles under tiny red peepers, and her loose-limbed groovy Ozzie kule looked a bit creaky. Felt pang of sympathy for her and couldn't help but think what joy this news wld have caused me only a few short months ago . . . but now I have eyes only for Adam.

Tue Nov 24

I am Appalled. Father has 'gone away for a few days' to get some 'space' and do 'research'. Mother doesn't seem to mind! *Wot* is this all about? I think with deadly chill of those pink envelopes and feel Horrified. I *knew* I shld have pinned him to wall and quizzed him about them. Have been so wrapped up in own puny Worries re werld fame and everlasting lurve that have neglected the real true Worries on my own doorstep. It's been obvious for weeks that Father has a gharstly secret. His nervous humming as he scampered to the doormat before me every morning . . . the Dread Pink Envelopes . . . shifty lukes whenever the phone went . . . I'm sure he's been spending longer in the bathroom . . . and what about that time he smelt of roses and wild flowers? And, oh God, Dolores. Crossword clue? Password to GOD? Pshaw. He is in lurve with some gharstly simpering nymph (or nimpering symph) barely older than *moi*self, who has him in her thrall . . .

Dolores probably adores him, thinking him to be wild romantick misunderstood artist bound down by shackles of family, who needs to explore wilde sexshual pashione in order to unleash his inner soul and write grate werks of art again. Arg. I know it's true. You read about it in the papers every day. Perfeckly nice normal emulsion-encrusted, haggard, paunchy blokes just vanish with sultry sirens, leaving swathes of weeping wives and children in their ruthless wake. True, these blokes are normally loaded, or else werld leaders Etck with all added magnetism of Power . . . but then Dad passes himself off as a writer, which cld seem V. Magnetick to pneumatick airhead.

I'm sure it's all my fault. I shld have been nicer to him, to them, to Benjy. Done a paper-round, helped out more at home . . . Arg. Gnash. Lash.

HOW can Mum seem so normal? Obv she is putting a Brave Face on it, hoping against hope that it will all turn out for better and that he will return to true lurve in bosom of her bosom. Well, if she doesn't want to tell me the Truth, I won't make her. Must be V.V.V.V.V. Nice to her and play Waiting Game.

Wed Nov 25
Babysit

Sleepless night except for brief troubled dream in which Adored Father tries to break news that he is Seeing Someone Else: *'Letty, you're old enough to understand, that when two people love each other very very much, there is no force on earth that can keep them apart.'*

'You mean like you love me? Or Benjy?' I say, *drawing a sword of blue flame surprisingly from my bejewelled scabard.*

'Er, not exactly . . .' stammers Adored Father as I smite him in two, carrying the nice half home to Mum and leaving the other draped in the arms of the cowering Dolores . . .

I have a DREAM...

Phew. What would Fred (sorry, Freud) make of that? NO babysitting as Only Mother stays in. I'm so Worried, that I keep flapping round her offering to make her cups of tea. She asks if I have gone mad. Maybe I have. Can't bring myself to bring up the pink envelopes. Have Deep Chill in heart.

Thurs Nov 26
Thanksgiving USA

V.V.V. Worried about Father. Resolve to find the pink envelopes. Maybe he left them upstairs in his 'study'. Feel bad about interfering in seedy, fumbling, glumey, drunken, fossilized underwerld of Parentz Emotions (how different to Pure, Leaping, Fresh, Decent Etck emotional life of Yoof). Do I dare go and luke? What more horrible thingz might I find?

Fri Nov 27
Film Course

Daniel Hope's Birthday (but who cares? Remember how I used to linger round card shops trying to find The One That Expressed Everything).

Film Course was really fun and even stopped me thinking about the gharstly departure of my beloved dad for a few brief moments. I played homeless person (I had asked Alfonsa Rosselini if I needed to bring in a costume, but she said I was fine as I was, wot a Worry). But still I found it hard to concentrate. The minute I got home, I crept up to Adored Father's cesspit of a study feeling V.V. Guilty and hunted feverishly in drawers.

Unbelievable. V. Diff to retain respeck for Moral Example and Major Roll Model when faced with the flotsam and jetsam of their lives. Combed through acres of old unpaid bills and bits of fluff and paperclips and tiny bits of flange and widgets and bus tickets and glue and nail-clippings and paperclips and wurzels and glunges and tubes and pots and spanners and nails and screwdrivers and batteries and lozenges and pen tops and buttons and newspapers and dusters and old birthday cards. Several times I saw a hint of pink. Once it was a Kleenex, once a ticket for a 1960s rock concert by the Crumbling Bones that looked as if someone had tried to roll it up and smoke it, once (heartbreakingly) a card from *moi*, when I was about seven to 'The BeSt DabbY in thE WErlD'.

And THEN . . .

. . . just as I was about to give up in glume at the state of my Adored Father's rume and therefore of his Life, I found it: a pink envelope, postmarked the 20th November. I opened it with trembling trembles. It was from David Springer! He of the briefcase-of-horror. It was a long list of clubs and bars with names like *Dykes Diner, Leather Lagoon* and

The Pink Triangle. It ended saying he would meet
Father on the 2.45 train and what a wonderful time
they would have and how brave he thought Father
was . . .

Yeech.

Father is GAY. He has run away with David.

He has left his family.

How can I possibly tell my Only Mother?

Sat Nov 28

Woke up in fever of anticipation, having plotted
into the night how to tell Only Mother the
heartbreaking news that Father has found his true
path in Life and that it tragically takes him from
bosom of only familye but how I will stand by them
both in this painful time Etck, Etck. Grone.

Stumbled down to kitchen intending to make
Mother cup of tea and found to surprise that she was
already up, and opening a pink envelope! She was
reading Dad's *mail*. All was lost. Heart in mouth
watched as I knew the dreadful news was about to
be revealed.

But no, it was a letter from Adored Closet-
Abandoning Dad (using his lover's envelopes, the
swine). Mum read it with usual vague smile
hovering about her mug. 'That's nice. His research
is going well. Sends you a hug,' she said, folding it
and slipping it in her dressing-gown pocket. God,

he's such a coward. Or is Mum hiding the truth from me? Should I say something? All I could manage to blurt out was, 'Why doesn't he phone?'

'Oh, he's in some remote highland place. There's no phone,' was my mother's airy reply.

The liar. I seethed, knowing he was haunting gay bars with David in Edinburgh.

'Anyway, he'll be back in a few days,' murmured Only Mother. 'Actually Letty, I was thinking of taking off for a few days while Dad's away. I haven't spent time at Mummy's for ages . . . er, and of course Granny Chubb could move in for a few days to look after Benjy . . . and you.'

Well, of course I muttered yes. I thought, my pooooor mother. She knows, in her heart, that Dad has left. She is going home to her own mother to weep and wail and beat her breast. She will gather strength at her mother's knee to break the gharstly news to her adored children before facing the werld as a Wooooman Alone. Arg.

Not that I cld see much comfort coming from Granny Gosling in these circs. She wld just congratulate Mother on Seeing Sense at Last, and start introducing her to widowed barristers and landed gentry. My hackles rose in defence of my poor father at the very thought. Must admit the idea of Granny Chubb being in residence for a few days always cheers me up. The floors gleam so that even Benjy believes they harbour no hidden monsters, the

fridge is overflowing with home-made apple
crumble, ginger beer Etck, Etck. At least we will
get a square meal.

Sun Nov 29
Advent Sunday

Mother scoots off to her mother's bright and early.
Tried to rob her dressing-gown pocket in middle of
night to see if Father had admitted all, but she had
removed the letter.

Why wld she have done that if it was as innocent
as she says? She obviously didn't want me to read
it . . . Am sunk in Deepest Glume. Realize I depend
entirely on having my folks around, like dreary
background muzak that they play in lifts and you
don't notice till it stops.

However, spirits lifted at the arrival of Granny
Chubb. The house was sparkling within minutes,
hot chocolate bubbling on stove next to vegetable
broth (today's cooking lesson – V. Good: how to
make V.V. Tasty soup out of a handful of old carrots
and beans) and all Benjy's clothes washed and
IRONED within seconds. I realized, as I smelt the
warm smell of freshly pressed pyjama, that I'd never
actually seen my mother do any ironing . . .

Peace shattered by Granny Chubb breezily saying,
'Must nip up and tidy out Popsy's study as a nice
surprise for when he gets back.'

'Oh, he hates it being tidy,' I gabbled, backing out of the room. Supposing Granny Chubb found another pink envelope? Not sure how she'll take the news when it all comes out (as it were), but whatever happens she mustn't find out like that. Hunted feverishly in Adored Father's tragedy of a study for more envelopes while G. Chubb diverted on way upstairs by sight of at least six objects she hadn't polished yet. Didn't find any pink ones but, stuffed into the back of his desk with a lot of final demands and ads for strawberry flavoured condoms . . .

Found one addressed to *moi*. It was stuck (chewing-gum, I think) to the back of a circular on double-glazed pizzas or something that must have been accidentally picked up by Adored Father in guilty haste to hide the pink ones.

Airmail.

Tiny sample of Parental flotsam...

Could it be . . . ? Could it possibly be . . . ?
YESSSssss. It was from Adam. Tore it open in wild flurry, forgetting everything else including hoovering, polishing presence of G. Chubb. It ran as follows:

Dear Letty,

I heard from Basil that you were hoping to see me the other day and I was touched by something he said, which I'd love to talk to you about when I see you.

I have had a bit of a difficult time recently and have lost my job (my own fault, really) at Mogul's studios, so will be returning to England on Saturday December 12th. Basil is getting something together at his place as a kind of welcome. It's nice of him considering I think I rather let him down before. It would be great if you could come. I really want to see you, so I hope if you can't make that day we get together very soon afterwards. I wonder if you still want to make truthful cinema? If so, there are very few of us left.

Affectionately yours,
Adam.

My cup runneth over. How typically restrained. How unlike the over-the-top romantick rubbish that Daniel Hope used to write (not a werd of it true). And what had Basil told him? That he thought I loved him? Oh, oh, oh. WHY do good things happen just when you're feeling terrible and terrible things happen just when you're feeling great so you don't know what to feel?

Mon Nov 30
St Andrews day (Scotland)

Aggy, as usual, a fountain of comfort and warmth
when she hears my news of Adam. Priscilla
apparently rang her last night but all she cld hear
was the twins squeaking, wailing Etck. Hard to tell
if Priscilla was doing the same.

When I got home, Granny Chubb was washing a
pair of fishnet stockings in the sink.

'Found these in Popsy's study, thought they could
do with a rinse,' she said, not at all surprised to find
them there by the look of it. The older generation
can be V. Matter of Fact about some things, and to
G. Chubb the most important thing about these
female undergarments was that they were an
invitation to clean something and thus make herself
useful, not that they were perhaps strange things to
find among her son's possessions.

But my werst fears were confirmed of course.
Obviously Dad has been wearing these under his
jeans for years and we never knew – but what did he
do when he got undressed at night?

I was much comforted by amazing fude, warmth,
glow Etck of family home, despite the fact that
several Large plukes have emerged on the end of my
hooter overnight, accompanied by first prickings of
cold sore. Cannot find cold sore wonder cream that
costs 5 million pounds per Chube. Can't afford to
get more.

Tue Dec 1
Period due

Time to check out my resolutions. Yeeeech.

Update Resolutions

1) Write in this diary every day
YESSSS! Is this a Teenage Worrier's Record?

2) Clean teeth twice a day
Have cleaned snappers ten times this week. Only
four times left out. Not qu fair though, as cleaned
them six times on Sun after trying some of Benjy's
Skunk Drops – foul new sweets wot are sweeping
primary skules in craze even bigger than the yo-yo.

**3) Limit spot, zit and pluke examinations to
once every two days**
Eruption of spotz, craters, pimples, zitz, plukes so
V. Grate today that this res obv not Fair in any
month in which I have a period.

4) Limit bazoom measuring to once a week
YESSS! Have NOT measured bazooms once this
week! Can do so now. Current measurement at 7.11
am: 30.9 inches breathing in V.V. Deep. Arg. Down

0.1 inch. How is this possible? Are bitz leaking out of bazooms and on to hooter? Filled with glume.

5) Only measure nose every month instead of weekly
Only measured once this week and not going to do so again, EVER, after bazoom experience above. If cld find way of reversing process above, might even, V. Shamefacedly, back experiments on animals if results like this could be guaranteed.

6) Stop reading krap magazines like *Smirk, Weenybop, Teendreems* Etck
Disgusted to read putrid interview with Candice Carthage in above, giving *Hollywood Beauty and Lifestyle tips* in which she claims to like older men. Yuk.

7) Read V. Good bukes to improve Mind, starting with *War and Peace*
Am now on page 12. Unfortunately, cover still reminds me of Adam, so I just gaze at it with tongue lolling out. Will Try Harder tomorrow.

8) Do homewerk on day it's set instead of whole week's werth on Sun at 11 pm
Now usually do a month's worth on Sun at midnite.

9) Improove speling
Irefutabutably.

10) Keep rume tidy
Will empty Vast Box tomorrow.

11) Be nice to Benjy
No. Am complete failure in this dept and left him
to clutches of gerbil-abusers . . . Must Try Harder.

**12) Save every speck of money for Granny
Chubb's Spectacles Endeavour (aiming to buy
her a pair for Christmas)**
No speck of money visible just yet, but babysitting
pittance will soon roll in. Maybe shld take up car-
cleaning again.

13) Stop being superstitious
Black cat crossed my path today and can't remember
if this is gude or bad, so maybe making progress on
this one.

**14) As above, cure one nervous habit each
month, starting with having to touch the floor
twice whenever I drop something**
Only touched floor twice eighteen times. Big
improvement.

15) Be nice about my mother's paintings
Now Father has abandoned us, must put Mother
first and be good to her in Every way.

16) Ditto about my Adored Father's writing
Huh.

17) Make New frendz
Not got V. Far with this. Everyone at film skule too
keen on own werk to show interest in *moi* and poss
new frend Priscilla now up to elbows in nappies.

**18) Do not wear same pair of socks more than
once**
Seem to be down to three unmatching socks. Must
check in Vast Box.

19) Keep Up with Werld Events
Overwhelmed by glume and dume of adult werld of
bombings, murder, torture Etck across werld.
Wonder if this is groan-ups' idea of example to
idealistic younger generation Etck?

**20) Add one new werd to vocabulary each day
as part of on-going Self-Improvement course**
Have done V. Well with this. Think will list them
all on Jan 1st.

Cold sore has now taken up firm residence just
under nose (like Hitler's moustache but with
consistency of stuffed crust pizza). Syd Snoggs greets
me with Nazi salute and Sieg Heil noises.

Wed Dec 2

Babysit

This note makes me V. Sad. It is such a short time since I wrote it, when we were normal happy family and I used to have wonderful evenings reading to my ickle bruvver while my beloved parents whined and dined each other in London's top nite spotz.

PC from Dad as though everything OK. Am astonished by mendacity of adult race. But cannot feel too glumey as transported on wings of lurve at prospect of seeing Adam. I have now re-read his note eighteen times. *'Affectionately yours.'* Swooooooon.

Thurs Dec 3

Period not come yet. Prob nervous tension as can't get used to dread feeling of Father possibly leaving home for good. How will it feel without vast festering piles of newspapers littering every corner of our hovel, no more emulsion blocking kitchen sink, no more bare wires coiling from unexpected orifices, ahem, no more manly voice echoing from behind locked bathroom door emitting deep groans as result of throwing up or lacerating self with pre-war razor, no more the comforting throb of Heavy Metal soothing *moi* to sleep, or the vibrant lektures on the struggle of the Werking Clarse to overthrow the

tyranny of Shopping? And, oh, no more cans of Old
Bastard Lager in the fridge. No. I won't have it. I
won't let him go. Have been wondering if I care
whether he's in lurve with man or wuman. Decide I
don't, just horrified he cld consider leaving us.

Look for clues when Mum phones – voice
trembling, blowing nose, stifled sobs, silences if I
mention Dad, orders never to fall in lurve with men
because All Bastards Etck, but nothing. She has iron
self-control, and my respeck for Only Mother goes
through roof. Or maybe she still wallows in the bliss
of innocence because he has been too much of a
coward to tell her . . .

Fri Dec 4
Film Course, 7.30

Cascade of spotz of remarkably varied sizes and
textures take some attention away from cold sore.
Still, shld be fading by next Sat when Adam back.

Fantastic evening at film skule. Alfonsa Rosselini
has decided to make my Kids in Rubbish pix the
centrepiece of the whole show! She sez, 'Letteee, zees
hearrt breakeeng peectures of tiny cheeldren asleep
on thee streeeets of London sum up so much that is
trageeek about our so-called ceeveelization. Eet ees
juss wonderrrrfool that you'ave caught thees
terreeble poverty in our own backyarrrd, when wee
in Europe theenk wee are so ceeveelized. Zeese

191

Keedz on ze Heeeeeep are like ze Flowers in ze Ashes, Garbage Cherubs . . .'

Methinks she is getting a bit flowery altogether for humble *moi*, but still appeals to Poet in My Soul, and I lurve the way she makes 'civil' sound like 'evil'. Maybe should cultivate husky Italian accent . . . She is getting posters made: *Six young film-makers tell It How It Is for New Directions*. And using MY pix for the poster!

I yam Over-the-moon. If this doesn't impress Adam, I don't know wot will. Re-read his letter 14 times to asswage any nagging doubts about his intentions. Over mune each time I scan its lustrous page. Also re-read David's letter to Adored Uncloseted Dad. Under mune, very.

Now **V. Worried** about something else. Period still hasn't come. Panic that Basil may have laced my drink and done unspeakable thingz to *moi* at party. I did get home V. Late . . . was there a missing hour in that grisly nite-of-guilt? Had I seen Basil again after he opened the door? Hadn't he loomed into the kitchen? Thank goodness for my trusty diary. Will re-read that bit . . .

Arg. Have found this grisly phrase: *Trapped in sea of surging bods for wot seemed like hours, feeling distinctly queasy. The vast form of Basil hove into view . . .* Could this have been the Dreaded Moment? I am no clearer, as of course if anything DID happen, I didn't remember it. That wld be just wonderful. You wait and wait for this Magic Moment and then can't even remember it.

And if he did . . . It wld mean investigations, statements, lawyers, social werkers, counsellors . . .

POLICE.

Cld I possibly, in my moment of anticipation of Lerve Redeemed, really be getting sucked into Whirlpool of Unwanted Pregnancy, assault charges, collapse of My Dreams (Basil is Adam's frend), spotty mug all over papers (DREADLOCKED DRUGS DEMON DRAWS DOZY DREAMER INTO DEN OF DUME)?

Now even sicker with Worry than before, and wish I had not kept stupid diary at all. Maybe I'll jack it in . . .

Sat Dec 5

Extraordinary day, really. Dad returned, breezily.

'Where's Mum?' he cheerily enquired.

How is it possible? Look closely at space between sock and trousers as he crosses legs in favourite armchair for signs of fishnet stockings. Only usual white hairy expanse. Shld I hold up newly-laundered items courtesy of G. Chubb and say 'Looking for these, by any chance?'

'Back tomorrow,' I say (between gritted teeth, not that you care).

He was obviously puzzled by mood of *moi*. Had I got out of bed the wrong side? Period, perhaps? NO, as it happens. Stormed off. Horrible werld. G. Chubb going. Father pretending life is normal. House descending into chaos around *moi*.

It is now midnite and I have run round block four times and been to bathrume eight times and **Still** no period. Of course, Idea of something happening at party just nutz. And yet, and yet . . . CAN you have sex without knowing it? Have seen tabloid stories of Gurlz in drugge-crazed sex orgies. Look at poor olde Priscilla. Still, the story goes about her that she doesn't know she's having sex even when completely sober and in the middle of washing her hair . . . No-one knew she was up the duff though . . . maybe she didn't even know herself? I am reminded of my pathetick youthful panic when I was fourteen and had my first kiss and thought I might be preggers. I was still V. Confewsed about the facts of Life then and although I know how it werks now, I've never had drinks laced with eville drugges before. Arg.

One gude thing, G. Chubb sez she will stay till Mon.

Sun Dec 6

3 am. This is fourth time I have woken up and been to loo to luke for period, so to speak. No sign. Now wonder if it really *is* possible something happened at that party. But if Basil had had wicked way with me he surely wouldn't have revived me with reviving water? Would he?

Arg. Might I have been consenting adult without being aware was giving consent?

Other alternative is periods have stopped for gude in V. Early menopause and I will live shadowy life blighted by childlessness.

6 pm. Have just read above and realized that Worries lume larger in glumey witching hrs of nite. As if I want children ennyway, when all I want is fame and fortune as creative *artiste* bringing peace to

195

werld. Period still hasn't arrived, but must be patient. Qu normal, sez my buke of symptoms, to have irregular periods at my age. Must gettalife.

Today, G. Chubb cuked me, Dad and Benjy the best Sunday roast ever. Sez she'll teach me Yorkshire pudding next week. She is V. Happy, singing and polishing and luking through photo album with Dad at pix of him on donkey Etck.

They always get cozy together like this when Mum is away. I sometimes think Granny Chubb wld like to move in and look after Dad just like when he was little. What with Granny Gosling feeling Mother has Married beneath her (or rather, and werse still, not married but shacked up with lesser mortal) and Granny Chubb feeling that my mother doesn't do a hand's turn, I feel our extended family is somewhat dysfunctional . . .

If Granny Chubb knew wot Dad had really been up to, how wld she react? Be distraught? Hard to imagine it, espesh considering the washing-fishnets episode. Praps she'd just start knitting frocks for David — and poss, for Dad too. He cld end up better dressed than he's ever been in his life. Strange thort.

Midnight. Period now nearly a week late. Calmness of earlier entry rings V. Hollow. Do not feel as though am getting period. But do want to wee all time, which is V. Well known sign of early preggers. Also nauseous. Shld I get a preg testing kit? Arg. I am like a seesaw alternating twixt dreams of byootiful Guyanese baby with dreadlocks and horror of obligation to bring Seducer to Book, or appalling choice of having little innocent visitor fostered. Increase of Worry Factor, fear of Adam's reaction. Madness beckons.

In my saner moments I'm sure Basil far too nice for this. But that is almost worse. Cld it have been someone else? Someone in the sea of surging bodies that engulfed me on that dread night? How long was I at the party for? Trouble is, the only witnesses to my return were two gerbil-abusers and a pissed five-year-old. I am overwhelmed that with all my vast knowledge of Family Planning Etck I cld have been so stupid. I have even carried condoms in my pocket!

And now something may have happened without my even knowing. Gharstly glume, irony, bed-of-nails Etck.

Mon Dec 7

NO sign of period.

But another pink envelope . . .

Faint hope that Father is mending his ways goes down plugge. Obviously, he has returned home for Christmas and will break the gharstly news to us after that.

'My darlings,' he will say, 'I have something very difficult to tell you. I have met someone else –

someone tall, dark, handsome, male . . .'

Mother will faint, ambulances will arrive. But I will fight this for the sake of All Our Happiness. First move: tie the frayed laces of his trainers to the banisters and DO NOT LET HIM GO. Then he will accuse us of having no understanding of the true meaning of lurve and say we are all homophobes. Second move: I will say, my best FREND is gay. And he will be amazed.

'Aggy?' he will ask.

'No, the byootiful Hazel, you prejudiced nit,' I will reply. 'And I don't care how much you lurve another, or whether it is man, woman or goat. You cannot abandon your only family to the slings and arrows of poverty and glume. You must stay here and face them with us.'

At that point, the Hand of God will come down from a thundercloud just like in ye grate Michelangelo's Sistine chapel ceiling. And the hand of God will wag its grate noble finger at Dad, and say 'Look after your kids, punk.' Etck.

Look after your kids, punk

Forced to quit this enjoyable daydream due to pounding on bathrume door. Emerge.

Must admit that in fact, parents have seemed mysteriously happier than usual lately. Cld there be a solution that doesn't involve separation? Maybe we could all live in harmony together WITH David? It cld be much easier on the domestick arrangements. All the clothes except Benjy's cld just be thrown into one big wardrobe. But then I cldn't start accusing my Adored Father of laddering my tights, and anyway, he isn't my size. Or maybe I shld forget their woes and turn my thoughts to Adam (not hard to do). BUT, arg, how can I when I'm probably about to have a stranger's child?

Spent all day at skule rushing to loo. Skulked round chemist's for hours on way home, too nervous to ask. Went into three different ones and bought a lip salve and two packs of lozenges (bang goes another £2.30 of my hard earned GCSE fund) before finally summoning up courage . . .

Tell you one thing I lerned from this: the price of a Do-it-yourself pregnancy test is Way beyond the reach of yer average puny Teenage Worrier. The woman in the chemist luked V. Sympathetick when she saw my fevered mug fall to floor and said, bring in a urine sample and they will do it on the spot. Fingered spots anxiously, but she gave me a plastic Chube. Felt terrible shame and angwish, as though whole werld luking at Just Me . . .

Is this wot poor old Priscilla was going through when I never had time to talk to her?

When I got home, period started like waterfall. Relief, dear fellow Teenage Worriers, knows NO BOUNDS. Of COURSE I didn't DO It with Basil or anyone else.

Mixed feelings. If I am absolutely completely two thousand per cent honest, there was in my heart just the teeniest pang, the minutest of fleeting twangs for my dreadlocked fantasy baby, and the nursery rhymes she or he would now never hear . . .

Must get Hed examined. Obviously the result of acute PMT.

I find I get PMT before, during *and* after my period at the moment, which leaves about one week free for normal behaviour, whatever that is. My Only Mother sez this will improve, only to come back with a vengeance at the menopause, which is not, as I once thought, a pause from men, but the Change of Life, when you stop having periods altogether and eventually become free to have Wilde Sex without complications, except for the V. Major complication that there is no-one who wants to Do

It With You by then.

How haaaard is the lot of women.

But will sleep easy for first time for week. Or would, if it wasn't for my father on brink of abandoning us in search of his new Lurve.

2 am. So much for sleeping easy. Pshaw. Rover in V. Odd scuffling mood and has kept me awake all nite. Has she picked up, with strange animal telepathy, my Divorce Worries?

Tue Dec 8

Thinking only of Adam and what to wear on Sat. At least it puts thorts of Adored Father leaping around in miniskirt with unshaved legs out of Mind. Was doodling dream outfit in maths but realized that had doodled Hazel wearing it. It is the person, not the clothes, that lukes gude, sad to say . . .

Wed Dec 9
Babysit

With Benjy as my dress consultant and Ultraworrying party looming on Saturday, etching acid fingers of fear into Humble El Chubb Brane, I spent evening trying on the whole of my and Mother's wardrobe.

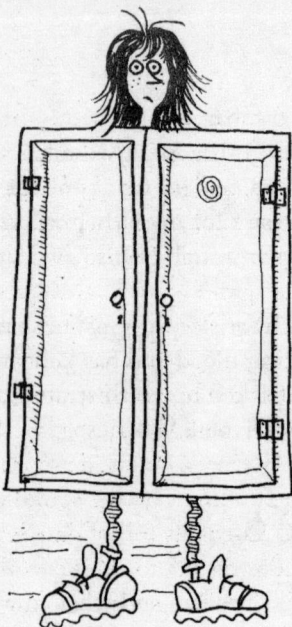

**Moi in wardrobe (no sign of
Narnia, sob)**

Hard to think of trying on a wardrobe without V.
Stupid mental Pic of spotty Hed crowned with
Spiky Wig jutting out of big wooden box, but you
know what I mean . . .

My own stuff, as faithful readers will know,
consists of a handful of tops and three pairs of
trousers, all in varying shades of jet, ebony, coal and
fog. Plus my trademark waistcoat, and a few boleros
and jumpers knitted by G. Chubb. There is also the
daring lacy slip in which, since my drunken orgy
and Single-Mother-Scare, I have somewhat lost
confidence.

Benjy liked me best in Only Mother's posh long gown that she got for Adored Father's buke launch twenty years ago and which she keeps in tissue shld another such occasion arise. It is indeed a magnificent gown – midnight blue and covered in dazzling little sparkly moons and stars, with a kind of silvery bridal train about 20 feet long. Is this supposed to trail along London's mean streets or be wound round bod like mummy? It smells of fresh flowers and feels slinkier than baby oil, but it is not quite Of The Moment. Wafted around in it for a few magical moments anyway, the sound of harps twanging and balconies full of daredevil hunks in DJs and tuxedos for me to choose from to fill my dance card . . . Decided such glamour was strictly for *Titanic* fans, and look what happened to Happy Ever After in that particular case . . .

As I attempted to slip out of said Glam Item, tripped on its frondy hem and crashed into the chest of drawers. Disconcerting ripping sound as I struggled to regain Edwardian ballroom poise, balance, Etck. A couple of fancy buttons had come off in the collision, so Benjy and I searched for them. I didn't realize he was clutching his felt-tip pen as a sign of authority until I saw the nice loominous pink colour ooze out onto the ball gown's pale chiffon train . . . I stuffed it back into five layers of tissue – Only Mother wld prob not wear it for another twenty years and anyway I could always sneak it out to the dry cleaners later, always assuming they had a Mad Baby Brother programme on their machine.

Glume descended. I couldn't go in a pair of black joggers and a mustard and lime-green bolero. Benjy suggested fancy dress and touchingly offered to lend me his *Star Bores* sword and helmet.

Then 'What about this, Letto?' he brilliantly suggested, fishing out my dad's only suit. Put it on. Must admit effect rather stunning. Loose, kool Etck, and only a V. few egg and beer stains on front. Will wear it. Adored Father will never know as hasn't had occasion to wear it since agent's party . . . I sneaked it off to my rume and ponced about in front of the mirror for hours. Wish there was one full-length mirror in this house, but I think I got to see most of myself by standing on different chairs and boxes.

NB Remember to go through vast Box before Christmas and get a little order back into my mangy existence.

V.V. Happy about the suit.

Thurs Dec 10

Period easing off. Spotz fading. Cold sore on wane. Happiness on wax.

Fri Dec 11

Hellish day at skule. Beaten black and blue with
hockey sticks, then given double detention for
doodling vast heart with arrow through it in my
Maths Buke. Prob if I had done Maths review sheets
also, would have got away with it, but I think it was
the very aloneness of the heart, without a single
accompanying figure or sum, that clinched it. Had
just started to add calculation of angle of entry of
arrow Etck to give **authenticity** (**new werd**: means
accuracy) to invasion of Maths Buke when Mr
Sphere rolled up, but to no avail.

But who *cares*? For I am AGOG with hope and
joy, on account of my artistick career getting better
by the second.

Haha. Alfonsa Rosselini asked me to come in on
Tue next week to do final edit. Will definitely
invite Adam to showing of films. Can't wait to see
final version of mine, which already lukes brilliant.
Sadly, there are no spare copies of the poster with
my fab pix of starving kiddies in trash Etck, so I
can't take one home and boast about it, but there
will be some extra ones next week. Alfonsa Rosselini
sed that because they are *real* pictures of *real* kids,
poverty stricken and probably sleeping out on the
freezing streets of London *tonight*, they give exactly
the right mix of hard-hitting social message Etck
plus Let They Who Are Without Guilt Cast First

Stone Etck, and should guarantee that the New Directions Course gets funding from the government for next year when she hopes we will all be back to make longer and even more gritty films. Of course, as is proved by my own Life (sob), cute starving kiddies pull heartstrings in way spotty starving teenagers (of whom there are zillions broke and tramping streets) do not.

Still, must admit I feel that my creative life is bubbling with promise . . .

Sat Dec 12

Sick with nerves re party. Managed to force down a single Galactic Snak. Hazel phoned in tears again. She's not allowed to go to Scotland this weekend, and now won't see Mandy till New year . . .

Shame innit, but I haven't seen MY true lurve for much longer, so I was a bit short with her. Then, just when I was settling down to really good Worry about how to do my wig, Aggy phoned to say the postman wants her mum to get a divorce.

Gharstly. It's bad enuf to walk out on all your hundreds of children (easy to lose count of all Aggy's brothers and sisters, but I think there are at least eight) without twisting the knife still further and divorcing all of them. *Oi! postman! No!* One must set some limits on parental abuse, I said to Aggy. I mean, how dare she get a divorce? It must mean she wants to marry the postman. I think this is truly disgraceful. Aggy is somewhat surprised by this.

'I don't care who she marries,' she weeps. 'I just want her back here!'

'What? WITH the postman?'

'Course not! But, you know, if she's staying away . . . (sob sob) then I spose she might as well marry him. Anyway, what are YOU so upset about? It's not YOUR mum.'

'No,' I sob. 'My mum and dad can't even get round to marrying each other. And now he's going . . . oh, never mind.'

'Oh no, not your dad too? He's never leaving?'

'No. No. No! Of course not!' I squawked, like chicken having feathers pulled out without anaesthetchick. 'Gotta go, gotta GO. See you at 7.30.'

'What?'

'You know, Basil's party for Adam. Aren't you coming?'

'You never asked. Anyway, I've got to look after Winnie and Charlie and Vaz and . . .'

'OK,' I grumped. 'See you.'

11 pm. Party woz nightmare, dear fellow Teenage Worriers in the vineyards of glume. I know, I woz there. You were not, so I'll tell you.

Arrived at 9 pm luking pretty kule.

Dad's big floppy jacket didn't luke too bad, I

thort, plus loose white shirt, loose flowing trousers that transferred wind-in-wig luke to wind-in-legs luke, tantalizingly ruffled wig to maintain element of former guise . . . Basil's house was athrob with the thunder of drums and the sound of laughter.

Took four deep breaths, felt faint.

Leant on door to recover and fell into house.

Saw huge form of Basil disappearing into kitchen but couldn't bear to follow as was overwhelmed by blushing inner shame at thought of the dreadlocked-dream-baby that never was.

Hall seething with sweaty bodies. Must be very careful not to drink any eville drugge-laced liquids or to fall into arms of passing lecher . . . Where was Adam? Stomach lurched with grisly feeling that he might have already left 'to babysit'.

'Ah, The Man Himself.' I hear a voice behind me. I turn to peer through the bodies at the front door. And there, yes, there . . . shimmering in all his God-given byooty, is the grape-curled winsome-limbed Adam. And, clinging sinuously to his muscled bicep is a six-foot tall supermodel with a mane of hair like a black waterfall.

How can I take this twice?

Blinded by tears, I staggered through nearest door, locked it and sat on toilet for wot seemed like days, stifling sobz. Even Basil, I thought, my only frend here after passing anxiety re Single Mother Worry, doesn't come to find me. I was so upset I forgot Basil didn't know I was there anyway.

People banged on the door and walked away at tragick intervals. Decided to make a dash for it. I just couldn't . . . I couldn't . . . confront Adam and his witchy paramour. Took quick glance in mirror to check I wouldn't scare anyone. Cold sore blazing like traffic light. *Smirkscreen* cover-up cream had given up against unfair odds and congealed into titchy white globules that clung limpet-like to the blazing scarlet pustule. Eyes like spiders stamped on by procession of 20-stone fellwalkers by now . . . suit obviously ludicrous, baggy, like Charlie Chaplin. Native American byooty on Adam's arm had hair like black ice, cheekbones soaring to frame haughty, almond-shaped, inky peepers. Chest like . . . well. I burst into fresh sobs. I unlocked the door, flung Father's jacket over my face, and bolted down the fetid hall and into the freezing night.

Am now toiling over diary, trying to make sense of all this. Have wasted months of my life hoping for something that can Never Be. Obviously, Adam just thinks of me as A Casual Frend, and probably just wanted to talk about my film-making. That's all his letter really said. Crazy of me to think anything else. Will now cry *moi*self to sleep in paws of belurved Rover.

Sun Dec 13

Spent the morning in bed with pillow over face.
Refused all food. Could not hold out after 3 pm and
lurked down deserted stairs to raid fridge. Empty.
Ended up eating whole packet of Galactic Snaks.
Felt minuscule amount better. How fragile is yuman
heart Etck that it can be cheered by Galactic Snaks.
Got my pile of skule library bukes, hot water-bottle
and Rover and hurled self into bed to concentrate on
ART. Phone rang constantly. Didn't answer it.

Mother put her hed round the door at about six,
carrying mug of cocoa. V. Touched. She drank the
cocoa and asked who Adam is? 'Why?' say I, heart
pounding like centipede on rollerblades.

'There are six messages from him on the
ansaphone, that's why.'

I raced downstairs, four at a time, new energy
flowing anew into my langwid form. Feverishly, I
dialled 1471 for Adam's number.

And rang it.

And this is what we said:

'Why did you leave the party?'

'How did you know I was there?'

'I didn't, until about midnight, then Junior said
you'd left early. Crying, he thought.'

'Who's Junior?'

'Friend of Baz's. Why didn't you come and see
me? Basil said . . .'

'What did Basil say?'

'Well, that he thought, you . . . er . . . l-l-liked me.'

'Huh!'

'Sorry. I was obviously wrong. Stupid of me to think you might. Bye.'

'No, wait . . . it's just . . .'

'What?'

'Well, I didn't know you had a girlfriend.'

'I don't. Candice chucked me. It was me or her dad. I thought I knew which way she'd go, but I was wrong.'

'Oh, and the Native American goddess?'

'Little Dove Wing?'

(Little Dove Wing. Yurk, thought *moi*, but held on to sanity for one second.) 'Yes. *Little* Dove Wing. Bye.'

I slammed phone down. *Little* Dove Wing. Great big hulking, slinky, bulgy, no-visible-means-of-support Dove Wing. I peered at the phone anxiously. Phew. He rang back.

'Letty. Listen. Little Dove Wing is a marvellous person. A fantastic film-maker too.'

'Oh. Great.'

'But she's just a friend. She's asked me to work on her new picture, which is about the genocide of the first Americans.'

(Arg. Wot is genocide? Must look up in dict.) 'I'm not as dumb as I look, you know.'

'Letty, will you LISTEN? It's true. She's engaged to Mario Paluzzi.'

(Mario Paluzzi. Handsomest hunk in Hollywood.)
'Really?'

'Really.'

'Oh, Adam.'

'Oh, Letty . . .'

Sweet nothings ensued. Can't beleeve it. Adam has been thinking of *moi* almost as much as I have of him. He thinks Candice, who is savagely jealous, has been sabotaging my letters. I am on cloud zillion, realizing at last that the True beating of my soul has found its just reward.

He's away all week clinching film job with Big Hawk, who's Little Dove's uncle and agent. But can we meet on Sat? I summon courage to say, any chance of him coming to see my first film. On Fri. Oh, he'd love to. Doesn't know if he can make it . . . will try like mad. God, he's, like, on his way to being a *producer* now. No longer the 18-yr-old boy luking for a break and dreaming. But still true to his roots, helping to make deep and Serious and Meaningful Films about Truth and Justice. Phew.

My JOY is unconfined.

NB **New Werd genocide:** meaning deliberate extermination of a people or a nation. So, this is wot the Americans did to the Indians (who are, of course, the *first* Americans) and what the Nazis did to the Jews.

Mon Dec 14
Hanukkah, first day

Another PINK envelope.

That's it. Enuf is enuf. I have to confront David Springer and save my lurved ones. I have to demand to know what he's doing trying to steal an unhappily married man from the bosom of his family? Left enraged message on D.F. Springer's ansaphone saying I didn't care wot he did, as long as he didn't steal lurving husbands and fathers from their rightful nest.

Shaking with fear at my courage, I soothed self by spending evening making costume of cloak, crown Etck for Benjy's skule play. He's playing one of the three wise men, har har. Found some old fake fur in a drawer and put big black dots on it with felt tip. Have rehearsed his werds with him every nite this week. He's got to say: 'Hail Mary, I bring thee Gold.' This is not a lot, I know, but it's a lot for Benjy who has never spoken before in any skule assembly and who always takes care to make himself invisible behind the tallest kids in his class even when he has to stand up there and shout the werds to a Christmas carol along with everybody else. This is always V. Frustrating for Only Mother and G. Chubb, who disrupt entire show moving around all over the hall tripping over people trying to see if he's akshully there or has run away in despair.

V. Excited about tomorrow, as am going in to do
my final film edit with Alfonsa.

Tue Dec 15

Fab time doing stuff with Alfonsa Rosselini. Dot V.
Kindly helped me with soundtrack. Think now got
it perfectly synchronized with Flowers in the Trash
(or Cherubs in the Garbage, or wotever they are) pix.
These, and the one of Granny Chubb with my infant
father, are now the central images of the film and
repeated several times. Must admit I found it V.
Mooooving, though I say it *moi*self, and think that it
will make audience ponder on meaning of Life, as in,

did we defeat Hitler Etck, try to make werld safer, more equal Etck only to tern our backs on our own people in relentless drive to do more shopping?

Tried to reach David again but no luck. Left message with whole list of reasons why Adored Father wldn't be right for him, eg Viz Etck that he drinks, he sometimes snores so loudly neighbours call Noise Abatement Dept, and that he isn't really interested in SEX of any kind because he can't stop playing GOD on the computer all day and night. V. Diff to contemplate saying things like this about Adored Father, but desperate sits call for desperate measures.

Wed Dec 16
Babysit
Benjy's skule Nativity play

Only Mother V. Upset this morning. Got call from big brother Ashley saying he has been invited to go ski-ing (again) with his posh fiancée's family. On the one hand good, she sez, if Ashley marries money it will be better prospect for dysfunctional Chubb clan than anything else currently on horizon (how materialistic can you get?). On the other hand, her only big gorgeous son will not be with us at Christmas. OR seeing my film.

Not that anyone cares about that except *moi*, it seems, sniff, boo. Thought of possible Christmas without either Adored Father *or* Ashley leads to lurching moment of self-pity.

Later, Only Mother awash with lurve, tenderness, joy Etck about Benjy's skule play. He akshully sed a whole sentence, which is a Big Breakthrough for him. It is weird to think that Benjy is so shy at skule when he's such a bundle of loveable (har har sounds of hollow laughter) tricks at home. Sentence Benjy spoke was, after long pause, 'Hello Sharon, I gotta gerbil.' Benjy had forgotten who he was supposed to be talking to or what he was supposed to say, so addressed the puzzled infant Mary by the only name he knew her by, and passed on the only bit of information that came to mind. Assembled shepherds, angels, donkeys Etck fell to their knees in hystericks, as did audience, so on the whole Benjy reckoned his speaking debut went pretty well.

Tried David again, without result. Leave following icy message: 'Coward.'

Thurs Dec 17

'There's a weirdo outside skule, asking for you, Letty,' sneered Syd Snoggs at the final bell. 'Looks a right wuss.'

Snoggs is V. Unreconstructed. News about Adored Father certainly gives El Chubb thorts she is not proud of, but that's only because it means that he is bound to leave us and it will not lead *moi* into the homophobic rubbidge of Snoggs and his ilk (NB ilk, New werd: meaning same kind of person).

Anyway, I couldn't imagine who wld be asking for *moi*, but of course it was David, who did luke a little unusual since he was wearing a bloke's three-piece suit, loads of make-up and high heels.

'I've got to speak to you, I can explain everything,' he hisses as though playing a Secret Agent in V. Bad film. 'Where can we go that's private?'

We stumble into a caff that's far enough from the one Snoggs's gang hang out in to be fairly safe and order two cups of tea. I am so frosty I hope tea will freeze over and really let Ludicrous Homewrecker know how I feel, but as usual Life is not like Hollywood Special Effects Dept.

But he does explain all.

First, he sez he is NOT gay. Feel first tingles of Major Confusion creeping up from the tips of my toes. He has lots of frendz who are, but he is qu . happily married with six children and just likes dressing up in women's clothes. Well, why not? He hasn't had the heart to tell his wife about it though. He holds down V. Respectable job Etck and feels if it gets out, as it were, people might not understand. Has to put army of offspring before principles re freedom-of-expression Etck.

Where does Adored Father come into all this then?

Research.

Research? Familiar feeling of being well and truly lied to overwhelms Chubb. Before have had chance to attach brane to hand, hand has werked on pure instinct and, in one smooth balletic arc, has poured tea over David's hed. Tea obv not even cooled by frostiness, judging by yelps of pain emitting from Springer. If I were in V. Bad movie above, or even in qu gude movie, I wld at this time have pushed table over and swept out into urban wasteland without backward glance, letting misunderstandings pile on top of each other to thicken plot, which wld end in ritual suicide of David, Dad and possibly Horace. However, this is real life and was so V. Worried that might have akshully scalded David that found self pathetickally getting wet towels from pissed off waitress and examining David's mascara-drenched mug for third degree burns. Both his mugs were all right, as it happened and, though shaky, he drained one of tea, which made *moi* rueful at waste of own beverage.

Had realized, of course, even as I poured tea over him, that he wasn't lying. And finally pieced together following stuff.

According to David, the hero of Dad's novel is a tortured transvestite who calls himself Dolores (wot else?) and who wants to tell his wife, but can't. Tried to get all this clear in spinning brane. Apparently, a Transsexual is someone who changes sex or wants to, whereas a transvestite is someone who dresses up as the opposite sex but doesn't necessarily want to BE them. It is a perfeckly good way, I now realize, for blokes to express their feminine side if they want to, and I must say I feel V. Ashamed of my ignorance over all this. Neither transsexuals NOR transvestites are necessarily Gay.

Dad wanted to visit clubs where people with this hobby go, but was too shy to go alone. When he met David with me the day he came to skule looking for me, he obviously clocked that David was a TV. Well, it wouldn't take Sherlock Holmes to figure that out. Anyway, by strange coincidence, he found himself in the Dog and Sporran that evening and David was there, trying to use the phone. Syd Snoggs's brother Dion 'Grotto' Snoggs was in there with his mates, and they realized David was a bloke dressed as a Gurl and were having a go. Adored Father akshully told them to eff orf and leave him alone, Grotto tried to stick one on Braveheart Father, who had been in the Dog and Sporran long enough to fall off his stool in attempting to square up to him, so Grotto smacked a hole in the mirror behind him instead and had to be rushed to hospital for a bludde transfusion.

I was amazed by all this, and my lurve and admiration for my Poor Misunderstood Dad, bravely standing up for freedom of expression, rights of minorities Etck knew no bounds. Anyway, he and David were chucked out of the Dog and Sporran for causing trouble and ended up in the Ant and Unicorn down the road instead, where they got even

219

more pissed and became firm frendz. In the course of this, the subject of Dad's buke came up and David offered to show him everything he needed to know. So Adored Dad rented a hovel somewhere near David's fave haunts and spent a week researching, getting filled in on the dress codes Etck.

I was V. Fascinated by all this and find I like David a lot. Have always thought it V. Unfair, as you know, that women can wear suits and ties Etck (like *moi* at Basil's party) but it's still a bit of a larf if blokes wear dresses. You can't imagine your headteacher coming in in a scarlet sheath and lipstick or even a neat jacket and skirt with slingbacks, can you? Not if your Hedteacher's a man, that is.

I put it to you, dear Worriers, that we can have a world leader who charms the people with a smile, a thong, and a cigar, but if he took it as far as making the State of the Union speech wearing a frock that wld be The End. Something tells me there is a V. Big prejudice here.

Anyway, I completely believe all that David has told me. Huuuuge relief.

Must say I Feel V. Glad I didn't blab to Only Mother re my theories about Dad's Secret Life. Shows it is definitely wise to keep one's trap shut sometimes and just wait and see . . .

David was V. V. Reassuring about all that. OK, so my Adored Parents had probs, who doesn't? He went on to say that my dear Adored Dad obviously

Only when above is routine will there be TROO
Equality (come to think of it, not many **FEMALE**
teachers dress like this, either)

adores all of us, and Only Way He Knows to Get
Out of Jail Free is to make this novel work, so we
can be Champagne socialists Etck instead of battling
for every penny.

Was V.V. Touched to hear this. Also, sentimental
at thought of Adored Dad in lonely flat striving for
Artistick Truth. My struggles with my film mean I
understand all this better than I did. Though of
course, Dad cld have just been thinking, Peace At
Last . . .

Can now breathe sigh of relief and luke forward to
Fab film course showing of my grate werk and
possibly – who knows? – even more fab meeting
with Adam, if not tomorrow, then Sat.

Fri Dec 18
Christmas Holidays
Film Course, 7.30.

V. Nervous about Film Show tonite. Something's
coming, something good, as they say in *West Side
Story*, but how cld they be so sure?

Sadly, Granny Chubb has V. Bad cold. Secretly
wonder if this just an excuse cos she is nervous, or
werse, upset, at me using her pictures, but banish
this guilt-making thort from brane. Benjy, however,
genuinely V. Upset not to be coming as Alfonsa has
banned under-twelves from seeing the films. If she
knew wot Benjy had seen at home in the company of

underage gerbil-abusers she wld be horrified . . . but my noble mother, father and loyal frendz Aggy and Hazel are all coming.

Feel inner glow at Lurve and support of Frendz. Skule was brillyont today, everybody giving each other cards, spraying snow spray and fart spray everywhere Etck. Carols playing, Christmas tree twinkling and Portillo V. Nearly smiling as he exhorts us to spend whole holidays under yoke of homewerk Etck. Why can't skule always be like this?

When I returned from skule, though, Benjy was throwing up. 'Not leave me with poooey babysitter! Will die!'

Mother in state of anguish. 'Oh, dear, he isn't well. Perhaps I had better stay with him.'

'WHAT? And miss my FILM?' I said incredulously.

Mother luked even more anguished with her 'torn-between-two-lurvers' luke that she always puts on when me and Benjy make conflicting demands on her.

As usual, Benjy won. I kicked him quite hard, when nobody was looking, as am quite certain he is putting it on.

'Letto kick me! Waaaaaaaah.'

'I did NOT,' I said, so convincingly that it made *moi* feel more shame than the kick.

Father, Hazel, Aggy and I surged off into bowels Etck of Chube. Car, as usual, terminally ill. Perhaps it's for the best, ecology Etck. One short journey in that car prob sets off fatal diseases in anybody within six blocks of exhaust pipe.

When we arrive, the studio is buzzing with people, wine, nibbles, and my posters are everywhere.

'Those are *my* pix,' I proudly cry.

The next three hours were a whirl of emotions. Everybody's film luked stunning to *moi*, and I couldn't luke at my own. Alfonsa Rosselini gave an **erudite** (NB New **WERD**: meaning V. Clever) speech and then announced that through the generosity of the Arts Funding scheme she was able to announce that the prize for the winning film is now £2,000.

Whaaaaat? Two *thousand* spondoogles? A gasp runs round the room and I can see my poor Adored Father's knuckles whiten as he grasps my arm . . . my heart goes out to him. Just think what we cld do with two thousand whole galabooshes free, gratis and for nothing.

Eet will go, continues Alfonsa, to ze most original of these six quite brilliant new films.

Just at that moment, the glass doors swung open and in swung Adam, a swirl of grape-like curls and a flurry of snow from his Armani-Versace-DKNY coat. He reached my side in one bound, which has always seemed to me a pretty hard thing to do until now.

He luked more ravishing than I had dreamt in my

wildest dreams, as though the pane and suffering of
his Hollywood Nightmare had etched a layer of
grater understanding on his hitherto boyish brow.
Phew. I longed and longed to hug him to my
humble bazoom, but instead introduced him to my
dad, who shot him a V. Beady luke. However,
Father's gaze more magnetically attracted to Alfonsa
Rosselini, who he was now surveying in manner of
famished mutt in presence of juicy bone. Was not
sure whether this was in hopes of only daughter
winning life-saving cash, or hopes of Alfonsa's
leaning over to expose abundant bounty in cleavage
dept. Whatever, she then proceeded to wax lyrical
about each film in turn. So-and-so's marvellous use
of blah, such-and-such's exquisite handling of blurg,
Etck Etck. Then, tantalizingly slowly, she glided
over to the podium to get silver cup and envelope
(presumably containing monumental cheque).

BUT, although she seemed to have gone into
incredible detail about everyone else, she had not
mentioned my film at all.

A dense cloud of Glume hung over me like . . .
well, a dense cloud of Glume.

'I will now award this excellent and well deserved
prize to the best film of all,' said Alfonsa Rosselini. I
cldn't listen. All I heard was 'for its blah blah blah
de blah and its amazing juxtaposition of blah de
blah and blah blah.' (It was a bit like a train
announcement, I realized. Could anyone else hear?
Was this buzzing in my ears alone?) 'And above all,

for the extreme blah di blah and ze breeeeelliant documentary photography of its maker, Letteeee Chubb . . .'

(SORRY?)

'I geeeve you a trageeck tale of our times zat exposes ze heeeepocrisee of our moderrn age and should make us all look deeeep in ourr hearrts and question zee deeeepest meeeeeeeening of ourrr lives, Letteee Chubb's *War or Peace?*'

All I can remember of the next few moments were deafening cheers (there were only about 30 people there, so they must have been shouting V. Loud or else I was delirious), a cascade of flashing bulbs (only the local paper and several people's Frendz . . . but, you know). And, being swept up by Hazel, Aggy, Dad and . . . and . . . Adam. 'You're a star, kid. See ya tomorrow,' he murmured, exiting in a blur of blackberry curls and lissom limbs.

Home, exhausted, thrilled, over-mune Etck to sleeping mother and peacefully snoring hypochondriac Benjy.

Happiness like I have never known: Artistick success and two THOUSAND juicy smackers. This will be one helluva Christmas: gold-rimmed specs for Granny Chubb, a bike for Benjy, a year's e-mail for Dad, oil paints for Mum . . . Who knows? Perhaps a ring for Adam . . . ?

Santa Chubb

Sat Dec 19
Ramadan begins

Over-mune-walking-with-winged-boots-and-
floating-on-sea-of-bliss about yesterday.

Alfonsa Rossellini rang to say she thinks the arts
board are going to put the film into the London
Film Festival in a new V. Short film slot for young
directors.

THEN Local paper calls to interview *moi*. They
are running V. Big story about *moi* and my film on
Monday. They are V. Impressed that local skule
(dear old Sluggs comp) has produced such, ahem,
talent. Reporter sez that the Flowers in the Trash
pic is going to be printed V. Big. Sez editor thinks
it's most stunning image they have seen for months:
innocent newcomers in the detritus of urban waste
Etck, which is perfect for Christmas, with homeless
people queuing up for cardboard boxes in snow
Etck, blah. He is amazed I found such little kids
sleeping out and wonders which bit of London it
was, but I told him that I had tramped lonely tubes
and streets every evening for months (slight
exaggeration, but I think poetic licence) taking pix
and can't be sure which were which. I went on at
some length about horrible poverty and my plans to
help werld's poor in future. Felt glow of self
satisfaction with job well done, but couldn't quite
bring self to ask if they wld pay me fee for picture.

Can't beleeeeeve all this.

I am all of a dither.

Had most Eckstatic evening of whole life with Adam, including Kiss of Kisses in which I liquefied like ice in volcano. We planned again our wonderful plans: to make films that will shake the world . . . together . . . Am seeing him on Tue. My Happiness knows no limits.

Sun Dec 20

Only V. Sad that Ashley not here, This will be first Christmas we have spent without him. But otherwise blissful weekend in bosom-of-family-values, pausing only to nip round to G. Chubb for kwick toad-in-hole lesson, which sounds V. Dubious but is V. Delicious and doesn't seem to involve either Toads or Holes, at least as far as diseased Brane of El Chubb understands them, or even Syd Snoggs for that matter.

G. Chubb was V. Sweet about my film and wishes she could have been there but was overcome, she said, by chesty cough. This is one of the V. Useful thingz about Old Age. You can claim being Overcome by chesty cough at the first sneeze and it can get you out of almost anything you think might be a Bit Much.

I give her one of the V. Big blow-ups of her original picture of her and my infant dad in the Blitz. She loves it, but asks for the original back.

Not sure I can lay hands on it, hmmm.

But will try.

Am feeling a touch Guilty about Benjy who
might not have been putting it on. He still seems to
have bad stomach-ache and has been lying moning
in bed all day. But I read him *Dr Eville and the Crypt
of Dume* and he fell asleep immediately.

Mon Dec 21

Woken by frantic call from Hazel. 'You're all over
the front page,' she chortles, giggling and jealous at
the same time.

Rushed to the newsagent and all the papers were
covered with usual old stuff – war, starvation, MPs
looking down gurlz T-shirts, vicars in knickers
Etck.

Blushed when realized Hazel must mean local
paper.

Yep, there I was. Front page news. There was an
enormous reproduction of the kids in rubbish pic
and a smaller one of G. Chubb in Blitz, holding my
dad in her arms.

The headline ran:

MOVING STORY OF
War or Peace?'
by Local Teenager
Did we fight two wars for THIS?

It went on to describe how I had singlefootedly trailed the length and breadth of the city to track down gharstly poverty and highlighted the terrible problem of homelessness 'movingly illustrated by the two unwashed infants asleep in piles of old newspapers'.

Course, I immediately raced back to show it to Mum.

Reaction was a little unexpected. 'But that's Bugsy,' she cried.

Er . . . what?

'I'd recognize that ring anywhere. And look, surely that's Duane?'

Sorry?

'Letty! How could you be so deceitful? You'll have to ring up and own up.'

Stomach lurched with dread lurch. Not a pleasant feeling as I'm sure you know, dear Teenage Worrier.

Grabbed the paper and, sure enuf, it is Bugsy and Duane. Only a bit of one face is visible, and they are both so covered in gunge, it wld be hard for anyone except their mother, or, as in this case, their best frend's mother, to recognize them. But the ring is a dead giveaway. There's no doubt about the ring. Why hadn't I noticed? How many six-year-olds wear skulls on their little fingers?

The horrible truth dawned.

It was one of the days I took pix on the Chube. Benjy and Bugsy and his little brother Duane had been making potions . . . we spent hours cleaning up . . . Benjy must have been fooling around with my camera and shot off the last few pictures at his horrible little mates, covered in potion and rolling about in the rubbish-infested, newspaper-strewn interior of Adored Father's Soul-Awakening Study.

Aaaaaaarg.

Flew up the stairs four at a time, shook Benjy awake and shoved the paper in his face.

'You idiot!' I screamed. He looked V. Scared and burst into tears.

'Tummmeee,' he wailed.

'Grow up,' I storm. 'This is where you learn how to be a Real Person. Face Facts!'

'Tumeee . . . Lettooo!'

Stomped out, desolate, betrayed, oblivious to the ringing of the phone and the ringing of the doorbell and the wails of my brother . . .

Only Mother charging up the stairs. She sed I must confess all. My moment of triumph dashed. 'If you won't ring them, I will,' she continued, ruthlessly. 'You'll have to give the prize back.'

'I CAN'T,' I wailed, more piteously than Benjy. 'No-one will ever know. It was a MISTAKE.'

'Maybe, but the pictures are fake. You can't get away from it,' she cruelly insisted.

Unfortunately the ring on the door was a reporter from the rival local paper, anxious to get new take on the local Teenage Tarantino-with-heart story. Father had just let him in. He overheard the row.

'Oh, the pictures were fake, were they?' he sneered, sneeringly.

'All a mistake,' I moan. Too late. The can of worms is open and the beans have spilled out. You know what I mean.

Loathsome Hack smiled oily smile of glee and fled into the dewy morning.

Oh no. How is it possible? The shame.

I ran from the house and walked, Lonesome as a Cloud, round Pigeon Poo Square.

I could not face cruel werld. And I still can't.

Mother says I have to own up, explain all and return the £2000. At least it's still only a cheque and I haven't spent any of it, except in my imagination.

I know Mum is right. I must try to get hold of Alfonsa Rosselini. But how? Wot will she think of me? Wot do I think of MYSELF?

Tue Dec 22
Shortest Day of Year

Just as well this is the Shortest Day of Year.

Can hardly bear to imagine how gharstly longer suffering wld be. The rival local paper has run the fake pix as a two-page story (knocking war, famine Etck off centre pages). The headline was SHAME OF TEENAGE HEARTSTRING CHEAT and the piece asked why public money was wasted on the likes of I when old ladies were dying of hypothermia . . . Arg. And, to my horror, the *Daily Scumbag* ran a tiny diary-type piece saying how the prestigious New Directions Course had lost its way and was handing out cheques to people who could only take snaps of their baby brothers' mates. Closer scrutiny necessary, higher standards, Kidz today can't tell Truth from Lies Etck.

Shame not yet complete. Worse to come, better believe it.

Anguished call from Granny Chubb. Two hacks from the local papers had been phoning up badgering her to ask if she was really the Granny in the pic and was it really the Blitz, or was that fake too?

Dad immediately phoned editor and threatened to duff him up if hacks bothered his mum any more. This side of Adored Father, defending Defenceless Etck, beginning to be V. Impressive, although now I fear price for his Courage will be story headlined: TEENAGE CHEAT ABUSIVE FATHER SHAME.

Rang Alfonsa Rosselini at Flash Escape studios. Incandescent with rage. V. Scary thing to listen to. She has sent out a press statement withdrawing my prize and is sure that New Directions will now have to close. Tried hard to explain but she just wldn't listen. Worse than her anger was her 'Terreeeeble sense of betrrrayal.'

Seconds after, Adam phoned, icily saying he wld prefer not to see me tonight, or ever again. I tried to explain but he coldly said he had a meeting about an *important, honest, worthwhile* project and put the phone down on me. So much for Innocent-until-Proven-Guilty. This is the Carefree Hero who fought lonely public battle against lies of Hollywood Moguls, struggled for Voice of Underdog Etck. Once he starts Having Relationship with Genuine Underdog, everything falls apart . . .

Feel Real Despair as I write this. I have messed everything up with a moment of carelessness. I couldn't remember taking the pictures, but of course I thought I must have done so. I had blocked out any self doubt cos everyone said how great they were. I had literally deceived myself into thinking I *had* taken them. And, of course, I honestly didn't think anyone else had . . .

I now have violent stomach-ache and am going to bed, even though it is only six o'clock. Benjy has been whingeing on all day about HIS tummy and refusing to eat so he can get sympathy and avoid being told off for STEALING my camera.

Rover is on *his* bed, as though she *believes* he is ill! Even my cat has abandoned me.

This has been the werst day of my life.

5 am. Oh God. I thought things couldn't get any werse. Mother woke me at 2 am saying she was calling ambulance for Benjy.

First time in my life I hadn't heard him crying . . .

Terrified, I leapt out of bed and we all hurtled off. Sirens blowing. Benjy white as ghost. Delirious. Moaning about Nice Floors. Cold terror for *moi*. Something wrong, definitely. Should have guessed, from Rover.

Accident and Emergency. Nurse took Benjy's temperature, and eyebrows shot up, hers not his. Not supposed to happen with nurses. Benjy was thrust into a wheelchair, rushed to a doctor and, almost immediately, rushed off to operating theatre. I sat with him and Mum and Dad while they gave him anaesthetic . . . and watched him fade into unconsciousness and wished and wished and wished he was laughing or crying or putting potions in my bed or stealing my camera . . .

They say they are pretty sure it's acute appendicitis. But what else might it be?

Oh my God, Benjy . . . I am sitting in hospital writing this. I can't believe how scared I am. The hospital is eerily Christmassy. They are playing *Silent Night* . . .

Wed Dec 23
Babysit

7 am. Have had a couple of hours' sleep in the waiting room. I feel so terrible that I would have been babysitting Benjy tonight. But I didn't listen to him.

At last some news.

Thank God, he is OK. They whisked his appendix out and said he might even be all right to go home on Christmas Day.

Feel completely numb . . .

Thurs Dec 24
Christmas Eve

Spent two hours Christmas shopping and bought eighteen presents for Benjy, using up all my money. I think he'll like the *My Little Boa Constrictor* best.

Then spent rest of day at hospital, reading *Fluff the Magic Puppy* and crying copiously. Benjy smiled weakly. I love him sooooooo much I could die. His bed has a little bit of forlorn silver tinsel wound round the bedstead. There is a very sick baby two beds down who moans all night. And a little gurl opposite who cries without stopping.

But there are other kids attempting to rollerblade down the corridors . . .

The nurses are Wonderful. It is V. Mooving, V. Sad and makes you think the only job in the werld werth doing is luking after the sick, poor and needy. Will revise my career plans accordingly.

Adored Father has been writing furious letters to local paper for pestering Granny Chubb. Am really Worried by how upset all this has made her . . .

Christmas card from David Springer, saying did

On second thoughts, maybe
El Chubb is not cut out for
caring professions...

those fishnets ever show up? Of course, they were
the ones I thought belonged to Dad . . .

Card from Daniel Hope asking me to New Year's
Eve party at his house. Think how excited it wld
have made me once.

But no card from Adam.

Well, I haven't sent him one, either.

My priorities have changed.

Spend evening wrapping Benjy's presents. Then
make him biggest card ever. It is a two-foot-high

snowman. I covered it in cotton wool (entire household supply, big trouble if medical emergency) and felt gharstly nauseous wave of nostalgia for when I made cards like this every year and everyone thought I was sweet and clever.

Fri Dec 25
Christmas Day

Snow falls. The house is strangely quiet. Benjy has always wanted a White Christmas.

And here it is. But he is not.

Dad and me went to the hospital. Granny Chubb and Mum already there, opening Benjy's stocking for him. His little face alight, carols, tinsel Etck. The Children's ward even more V. Moving than before since all but the very ill have gone home for Christmas Day . . .

We are allowed to take Benjy home for Christmas dinner.

I am truly amazed, and deeply touched, to find my parents have bought me the coat I yearned for.

'B-but I've got one,' I say, feeling odd wave of fondness for the nylonette-Coat-of-Glume that has seen me through such pain and anguish.

'Yes, but you hated it,' they chorus as one.

Benjy is the centre of everyone's attention, especially mine. Briefly ponder how annoyed this wld've made me a few short daze before, and now I

can't do enuf for him. We take him back to hospital
at 8.00. I want to stay overnite, but Only Mother
can't keep herself away, even though we know Benjy
is not in danger now. We leave her sleeping on floor
by his little bed and return to sit in front of telly
with paper hats on, feeling cosy. I put on the new
bolero knitted by Granny Chubb. She has surpassed
herself this year with a colour combination of lemon,
maroon, pale green and a strange colourless colour
somewhere between biscuit and mushroom. She and
Dad giggle over photos as usual, nearly, but she
seems a little, well . . . wistful.

Sat Dec 26
Boxing Day

I now know the law of coincidence is stacked against
moi.

At ten o'clock, just as Granny Chubb, Dad and I
were getting ready to go to the hospital, the
doorbell rang.

It was Adam. Wouldn't it just be? He said that
Aggy, who he met at Basil's Christmas bash, had
told him the whole story about how I thought I had
taken the pix. He said he thought I'd been daft, but
he understood. He said he knew, from bitter
Hollywood experiences, what the 'gutter press' (he
means the rubbish papers like *The Scumbag*) are like
and how they distort the truth. Feels V. Sorry for

me. Maybe, he seemed to be about to hint, we could try again.

But just at that moment as, my jaw dropping, I attempted to form werds, the bell rang again.

It was nerdy Brian, staggering under monumental bunch of wilting roses, wanting his hanky back. And he was closely followed by, no, oh nooo. Daniel Hope. Armed with balloons and a bouquet the size of Alexandra Palace.

Adam went pale as lilies, then fiery as fire, then blacker than thunderclouds, then cold as stone. He turned and marched away.

'Wait, I can explain everything!' I shouted, like in a bad movie.

'Too late this time, Scarlett,' he sneered, as if in a werse one. 'First Daniel Hope, then your absurd jealousy of Little Dove Wing, then your pathetick fake pictures, now Daniel Hope again. And another boy who seems to know you VERY WELL. Hanky indeed. Tell that to Othello!' And off he stormed, his curls flying.

I have no idea wot this hanky stuff is about, but realize this is my last chance. I zoom down the path after him.

'I haven't seen Daniel Hope *at all, till now*. I can't *stand* Brian. I want YOOOOU.' But my werds are blown away by the icy gust, lost in the howling snowstorm as Adam leaps with one bound (how does he DO that?) on to the only bus in London and sails out of my life. My werds are lost. All is lost. Adam is not the type to change his mind again.

I threw Brian and Daniel Hope's flowers into the snow (Granny Chubb rescued them and brought them to the hospital). I yelled and cursed (Granny Chubb looked deeply shocked). I was deaf to anything but the sound of my own heart breaking.

Sun Dec 27

Woke cursing the bitter unfairness of my Life. It is SO unfair. How COULD Brian AND Daniel Hope BOTH turn up at the same time? As ADAM? There was a scrawl from Daniel Hope on the door mat: *Sorry, bad timing. Just passing and wanted to check you could come to the New Year's Eve party. The flowers were for my mum. Pretty pissed off you chucked them in the snow. But no hard feelings. See you on the 31st.*

I felt like killing him. To think I once thought his hair was like wet sand in sunset when it is quite obviously just the colour of old brown envelopes.

I had to talk with someone, and poured my heart out to Granny Chubb this morning as she was showing me how to scrape a carrot without hurting it. I told her everything, even the Truth about the pictures. She was kindness and wisdom itself but quite suddenly, and to my dismay, she started to cry.

I had never seen her cry before and was quite overwhelmed.

'What is it?' I tenderly asked, feeling rising gulp of compassion, and after a little while of coaxing, she told me.

She was crying about the photo of her in the Blitz. The one whose original was lost, but which I had got fab copies of that I thought she had been so pleased about . . .

The child in her arms was not Dad, but her first child, who had been killed in the Blitz. She has not been able to talk about it to anyone except Grandpa Chubb, all these years . . .

So Father had an older brother he never knew about?

No. Father did know. It was an old family tragedy that he had kept to himself, as he knew Granny Chubb preferred it that way. I thought of Dad's knuckles whitening as we watched my film. And I thought it was just about money . . .

And now I understand why Granny Chubb is so sad. That original photo was like a real link to the baby. The baby probably saw it and may even have touched it. Grandpa Chubb would certainly have touched it. It was a memento that was more than just an image.

Mon Dec 28
Bank Holiday

I spent all day in hospital, trying to make self feel

better by comforting Benjy. Vast craters of spotz
emerge on cue, as usual. They will be like mountain
range by the time of New Year's Eve party.

Tue Dec 29
Period due. Or is it? Last one nearly a week late . . . so
maybe this one shld come in six daze to get back into
nature's cycle, rhytmn of yuniverse Etck

Period comes accompanied by cascade of spots,
including large one on my bum, which makes it V.
Difficult to sit down. However, since No-One In
My Life likely to get close View of Same, could be
worse.

Or better.

Decided to finally tidy rume in slow attempt to
crawl back to land of living, gain self respeck and to
be a Better Person. So I emptied contents of Vast
Box. What fell out of the flap? Dad's synopsis.

Coincidence in my favour for once. Will make
such a brilliant Birthday present for him (and free). I
feel almost happy for a few moments. And express
this by making another giant card, this time for
Dad. Have chosen rather novel (ahem) idea of
making card luke like buke jacket and called it:
V. GOOD BUKE by BEST DAD IN WERLD.

Hope he will be pleased, and think, there is
always some solace in creativity, no matter how low
your spirits are . . . V. Hard not to tell him about

synopsis, but have decided it must be his treat for
tomorrow.

Wed Dec 30
Father's Birthday
Babysit (No, doing this on Fri for parents to go out for
Dad's birthday treat)

My father has always said kids are spoilt these daze
and get too many presents and that when he was a
kid he and Granny Chubb used to huddle around a
cheerfully crackling match, while he excitedly tore
open his single present, perhaps a shiny new penny,
or a scraping of soap.

   So today we pushed the boat out for him. Benjy's
illness has taken its toll. He has luked completely
ashen for daze. So, first-and-best-surprise was
Benjy's homecoming.

   Close second was the synopsis, which I had
wrapped in sixteen lots of paper and then put in
Vast Box (unfortunately, contents of box still strewn
all over my floor, cos wot with making Father's card
and then wrapping his present I didn't have time to
tidy it all up). At first was Worried he might think
that box contained fab new komputer stuff, but V.
Releeved when I saw the luke of unadulterated joy
on his poor wrinkled brow. He even gave me a hug,
something he has not done much of recently since
reading about father carted off for child abuse after

245

kissing daughter in public place. Mother had signed him up for a month's free e-mail subscription and sez she will pay for next three months. She's also taking him to theatre on Fri.

Granny Chubb cooked Birthday feast of Dad and Benjy's favourite fude (ie: roast chicken, Yorkshire pud, chips, baked beans, pizza, roast potatoes, carrots with brown sugar, Smarties, mandarin oranges, condensed milk, chocolate ice-cream and Strawberry Angel Delight). I was not complaining. I had deep talk to Granny Chubb, who is staying over New Year, about her secret.

It weighs heavily on me, but I know she told me to comfort me and to show me that not only cameras, and newspapers, but even people as apparently perfect as her can be economical with the truth.

Thurs Dec 31
Daniel's New Year's Eve party

I made a surprising decision today. I decided not to go to Daniel Hope's party. Aggy was astonished. But I felt it wld be too painful to see other Teenage Worriers flirting and letting hair down Etck and that I have too many fresh wounds to nurse.

Decided instead to see the New Year in repenting my sins and to write a long letter explaining exactly what happened to Alfonsa Rosselini, begging her to

take me back on the course next term. Have
returned the cheque already, nachurally, with a
grovelling note of explanation (toiled over by my V.
Kind Adored Father) to the Arts Funding Board. I
can only hope it bears fruit. Maybe when she's had
time to kool down, Alfonsa Rosselini will
understand . . . Also wrote to Adam, not in any
hopes of winning him back but just to, well, tell
him I didn't lie.

Have been thinking hard about all this because,
well, I did in a way. I could never remember taking
those pix. If I'd only thought harder . . . Also, didn't
care enuf about Hazel, Aggy, Benjy, Granny Chubb
or anyone else. Shame and guilt mingle in equal
measure . . .

Have dipped into the real *War and Peace* from
time to time this week. It has shown me that Adam
and *moi* are like earth and water: fine separately, but
like mud when combined. Tolstoy writes like this
about Napoleon's army invading Moscow. He also
talks about the soldiers looting the city (and
destroying themselves). He sez, it is like when a
monkey puts his hand into a slim-necked jar to get a
handful of nuts but, when he has paw clenched
round the nuts, he can't pull it out of the jar, as the
neck is too slim. So he dies. It is only by letting go
that he can be Free.

It's a lesson. So I will Let Go of Adam. I will
pursue my Art, my skulewerk and my frendships. I
will be true to those who care for *moi*. I will learn all

247

about the other festivals and kulchures that I haven't bothered about. Succoth, Hannukah Etck are Jewish ones, which makes me feel even werse about exploiting the war for my own pathetick vanity.

I am even thinking that I shld start to really grow up and use that werd about dying that rhymes with breath. Next year, I will. Granny Chubb's experience and my fears about Benjy have made me see how V. Childish I am . . .

9.30 pm. Ahem. All this deep thinking has not stopped *moi* from bitterly regretting decision not to go to party . . . Am imagining all my frendz kissing each other under mistletoe, singing *Auld Lang Syne* Etck. Will go. Just for hour. Just to say Happy New Year to Aggy who is gude frend and werth a thousand Adam Stones. And to Hazel who is V. Upset not to be in Scotland with Mandy.

1 am. Unbeleevable evening. Shows that when you don't bother, stuff can happen, I think. Tore out of house without even changing clothes . . . (Adored Father agreed to give me a lift, just to see New Year in, although insisting on picking me up at 12.30 . . .)

Got to Daniel's house at 11.55. Not AT ALL nervous, as don't care about Daniel and knew Adam wldn't be there. Saw Hazel and Aggy in midst of throbbing throng. 'Hazel! Aggs!' My dear frendz. BUT, behind them loomed . . . a laughing Boy. He was . . . about five feet 10 inches tall, eyes a mix of sea-green and ocean-blue, very dark but with flecks of gold in, you know, a bit like a sea tossed by the wind with floating specks of sand catching the glinting sunlight. Soft thick hair, the colour of, wait for it . . . vanilla fudge . . . Straight nose, aha, with just the teeniest little bump in the middle, chiselled type jaw but, you know, not boringly chiselled like Action Man, with a curly sort of mouth in a broad smile, a little dimpled cleft on either side, long neck but not too long, broad shoulders tapering to a narrow waist with a neat bum, but quite pert and long legs, very straight. Complexion the colour of toffee fudge . . . tiny scar on his left cheek, in the shape of a lightning flash . . .

In short, none other than Mystery Boy.

'My God, that's him,' I squeaked.

'Who?' chorused Aggy and Hazel, bemused.

'Mystery Boy. That's him.' I was jabbing the air hysterically.

'But that's . . . just old Basil,' said Aggy.

'Don't be daft. Basil's eight foot wide with dreadlocks.'

'That's not Basil. That's Junior. He's Basil's flatmate. Look.' I turned to see the vast bloke I'd assumed was Basil. I felt faint.

'You mean, that amazingly kind bloke with the melting chocolate voice who told Adam I lurved him was not a 30-year-old dreadlocked bloke built like a barn but . . . but . . . Mystery Boy?'

'Spose so.'

'Why didn't you TELL me?'

But of course, there was nothing to tell. Aggy had known Basil since she was three. She hadn't connected my description of Mystery Boy with her old pal for one second.

'I'll introduce you, to make up,' she winked.

'NO, NO. YES.' Sudden thort that had not changed clothes, luked like raddled pasta Etck overwhelmed *moi*. 'No. Look, Aggy, just tell him I was here, right?'

The bells were chiming. A fat sweaty bloke on the TV was counting down from ten.

'Basil, this is Hazel and Letty.'

Dongggg, Dinggggg, Donggggg . . .

Basil: We meet at last.

Me: Myaahsplurfnnnnaaaahhahaha.

Basil: I feel we've met before.

Me: (Help. Does he remember that apparition-with-marmite outside the skule loo?) Nyaaark. Splafffft. Yukkanurk.

Dingggggg . . . dongggggg . . . dingggggg . . .

Fri Jan 1
New Year's Day

Woke to discover snow crisp as snow on ground. I felt a strange lightening of the heart as the New Year dawned.

But of course, dear reader, my heart is full of . . . Basil. That this young God can go by such a name is beyond me, but that's life. We were whirled apart by the dancing throng last night. But he smouldered and *definitely* blew me a kiss. And I feel, in my bones, that we Will meet Again, as if destiny's threads were weaving us together . . .

BUT, I won't be deterred (famous larst werds) from my Art. And I WILL contain my seething passions. Yesterday's resolutions will NOT be undone in a single Day.

Was just thinking this when heard anxious tones of my Adored Father (getting ready to go to posh theatre first nite on arm of Only Mother) . . . 'Where's my suit?'

Accompanied by enraged voice of only Mother: 'What's happened to my *dress*?'

Yeeeeech. The suit. Scrunched up under my bed . . . the button-free ballgown, decorated with Benjy's felt-tip . . . It seems there is some way to go before the conscience of El Chubb can meet the unending demands set by Life Itself.

Whatever That Is.

The End

(for now...)

POSTSCRIPT
UPDATE... RESOLUTIONS

1) Write in this diary every day
YES. Will now begine New Diary and see if I can keep it up (as the art mistress said to the gardener) for a whole year.

2) Clean teeth twice a day
More or less on target, given bathrume and mirror crisis and fact that no-one ever buys toothpaste and fact that my toothbrush now lukes like mangled porcupine, only more fuzzy.

3) Limit spot, zit and pluke examinations to once every two days
Only gude thing about gharstly crises of last weeks is that I have had V. Little time for these ordinary Worries. Does this tell me something about werld?

4) Limit bazoom measuring to once a week
Back to usual measurement at: 31 inches breathing in V.V. Deep.

5) Only measure nose every month instead of weekly
V. Good. Did not measure ONCE this month.

6) Stop reading krap magazines like *Smirk, Weenybop, Teendreems* Etck

Must admit, bought all three last week. Was far too glumey to read anything else. Am now an expert on this year's fab Winter makeovers, hairdos, appliqué underwear and New Young Stars of stage'n'screen. Also terminally bored with all the above. Wonder if it might be possible to invent an Interlekshual magazine for yoof about environment, muesli, Tolstoy Etck. Yawn.

7) Read V. Good bukes to improve Mind, starting with *War and Peace*

YES. Have read lots of bitz of this. Will read all of it this year.

8) Do homewerk on day it's set instead of whole week's werth on Sun at 11 pm.

Total failure, glume Etck.

9) Improve spelling

YES. Have just luked up 'improve' and 'spelling'. V. Embarrassed. Tempted to re-write earlier resolutions but realize that this wld be dishonest and like rewriting history. Will try to use dikshinonary from now on.

10) Keep rume tidy

Er . . .

11) Be nice to Benjy
Gulp.

**12) Save every speck of money for Granny
Chubb's Spectacles Endeavour**
Treble gulp, failure, glume.

13) Stop being superstitious
Friday 13th in these three months was indeed werst
day of my Life. But am determined to see this as
coincidence and anyway, Sunday Dec 13th was V.
Nice. Not that it lasted, but then life itself doesn't
last, does it? Sob, mone, grone.

**14) As above, cure one nervous habit each
month, starting with having to touch the floor
twice whenever I drop something**
In the midst of my current confusion and pane, I do
not think I am strong enuf to tackle this V. Big
One.

15) Be nice about my Only Mother's painting
Have paid no attention to Only Mother's Art
whatsoever. Do I care enuf? Must Try harder.

16) Ditto about my Adored Father's writing
At least I found his synopsis. But then, I also lost his
synopsis, by stealing his Vast Box. Guilt, shame,
Worry and Pane.

17) Make New frendz
NO. Be More Caring about the faithful frendz that I have got.

18) Do not wear same pair of socks more than once
Now seem only to have one sock. First Christmas ever I was akshully hoping to be given a pair . . .

19) Keep Up with Werld Events
Wot can I say? We have bombed Iraq and I was thinking of Adam.

20) Add one new werd to vocabulary each day as part of on-going Self-Improvement course
Have done V. Well on new werd front, but what does it all mean?

Seems to me I have over-indulged in *faction* by combining fake pix with real ones to detriment of Career and Soul, not to mention *authenticity*. Obviously I have lukes of depraved *beatnik*, mind of *dilettante*, am likely to end days suffering from *lumbago* due to krap posture, have found out V. Few *salient* facts, have found Life far from *dulcet*, have suffered almost *unadulterated* glume − except for brief bouts of meaningless *euphoria* − am living *parlous* existence, a positive *roux* of *dolorous* events which show V. Little sign of *abating*, cannot overcome endless *psychosomatic* symptoms and their

255

ilk and am, in short, being far from *erudite*. V. Unlikely to have left anything werthwhile for *posterity*. At least, I can be determined to fight *genocide*.

And, on liter note, have invented, with help of Benjy, following new werds which hope will enter langwidge with YOUR help, dear reader:

Flurg (for stuff in bottom of your pockets)
Skangdoogle (for weird objects you find in drawers but don't know what they are)
Skank (anything nasty)
Ploomp (anything soft)